Mine Intercom Messages from the Realms of Light

The Great Awakening Volume X

Sister Thedra

ISBN: 978-1-7363418-8-9

Contents

Mission Statement

Give the truth to the world. Let it be received where it will. Many will read the messages. Some will accept the truth, others will read through curiosity, a few will ridicule. Yet to all is the truth given, and to all remains the power of choice.

The hope of the world in these times is in spiritualizing all forms of activity---promoting understanding through love and service. These must be the watchwords if the world is to come into lasting peace. We are trying to influence a world that is going astray and could cause undreamed of suffering. We are trying to overcome the thought of materialists and to bring a spiritual outlook into the earthly life. We need the help of all on earth who can think in spiritual terms. The great battle to be fought now is between the spiritual and the material, between idealism and carnalism. You can help by spreading the word---we are asking that you help because the battle may be long and the victory far away.

Halls of Light is not allied with any sect, denomination, political entity, organization, neither endorses nor opposes any cause. There are no dues for membership. Halls of Light is self-supporting through its own voluntary contributions. Halls of Light has but one purpose: to help through encouragement and understanding...

To contact the publishers or to obtain copies of our other books, please contact us at email: goldtown11@gmail.com

Esu Jesus Sananda

This reproduction is from an actual photograph taken on June 1st, 1961, in Chichen Itza, Yucatan, by one of thirty archaeologists working in the area at the time. Sananda appeared in visible, tangible body and permitted His photograph to be taken.

About the Late Sister Thedra

Since the later part of the last Century the Kumara wisdom preserved by Aramu Muru has begun to reemerge into the world. This process began with the late Sister Thedra, whom Jesus Christ appeared physically to while on her deathbed and spontaneously healed her of cancer while she was in the Yucatan, where she had gone to accept her fate, and the will of our Lord Jesus Christ. That is when something miraculous occurred.

Jesus spoke to her saying, "My name is Esu Sananda Kumara" and then sent Thedra down to the Monastery of the Seven Rays to learn the Kumara wisdom.

After five years, Thedra was told to return to the United States where she founded the Association of Sananda and Sanat Kumara at Mt. Shasta in California. While heading this organization, Thedra channeled many messages from Sananda and taught the Kumara wisdom until her passing in 1992.

While in the Yucatan it is said that while Sister during the 1960s Thedra was in the Yucatan, she was told a secret by her friend George Hunt Williamson, also known as Brother Philip, who authored Secrets of the Andes, and the SECRET PLACES OF THE LION. Williamson, confided in his long-time friend Sister Thedra that he intentionally scrambled the reincarnational lineages in order to protect this next generation when they the Mayan Solar Priests, who were the direct line descendants of the Kumara according to prophesy were scheduled to reincarnate or return to fulfill their missions upon Earth, one of which was to relocate these ancient sites where the original records of the Amaru were placed for safe keeping.

Sister Thedra, 1900-1992, spent five years at the abbey undergoing intensive spiritual training and initiations. While in South America in the Yucatan, she had an experience which changed her in an instant when as it is told by her that Jesus Christ physically appeared to her and spontaneously cured her of cancer.

He introduced himself to her by his true, name, "Sananda Kumara," thereby revealing his affiliation with the Venusian founders of the Great Solar Brotherhoods. It was by his command that Sister Thedra went to Peru where in here travels she met Williamson. Sister Thedra eventually left Peru upon telling her experience there was complete.

Even before she returned to the States she met with harsh criticism from the church, which she elected to leave. (JW That was the church that is in Salt Lake City, Utah.)

She then traveled to Mt. Shasta in California and founded the Association of Sananda and Sanat Kumara. A.S.S.K.

You ask, Is There A Difference Between Jesus and Sananda?

Our Lords name given at birth by his father Joseph, and his beloved mother Mary was Yeshua, thus being of the house of David and the order of Yoseph, he would be called Yeshua ben Yoseph.

The Roman Emperors placed the name of Jesus upon the sir name of Yeshua, after the Emperor Justinian adopted Christianity as the official faith of Rome, and ordered that the sacred books be compiled, upon approval of a specially appointed council, appointed by the Emperor, into a recognizable and uniform work titled The Bible. Prior to this there never was a Bible per se.

There existed until the time of the Emperor's edict, a selection of many Sacred texts, that were employed in the Sacred Teachings. Many of which were copies of what the Greeks had transposed from the original texts in the Libraries of Alexandria, which were originally compiled by Alexander the Great, and were destroyed by Julius Caesar, fearing that they might prove dangerous to the rule of a Caesar, an Earthly God.
In addition, it kept. (he thought) the knowledge of Alexander's Libraries, out of the hands of the Ptolemy's, who were said to be descended from his bloodline.
At the time Caesar had no way of knowing the vast portions of the Library that were already in the Americas, in the Great Universities of the Inca, and the Maya.
Yeshua spent many years in the East after his ascension.
The good Sheppard, upon his appearances to the

Apostles after his ascension told his Apostles that he was in fact going to tend to his Father's other sheep; which means, plainly that he was continuing upon his sacred journey.

As the ascended one, Yeshua took to himself the name of Sananda, meaning the Christed one, and Sananda was thus embraced forever more by the Great Solar Brotherhood.

To many of you this is all new, to others it will be received as a welcome easing of the wall that has so long separated two sides of the same coin, this is being placed into the ethers and the matrix of thought at this time as it is the time of the Awakening, and the Christos is already emerging into the new consciousness, and mother Earth herself.

Sister Thedra and the phenomenon of channeling. Authority to use the name of Sananda was given to Sister Thedra when Jesus~ Sananda appeared to her in the Yucatan, and cured her instantly of the cancer that had taken her body over. Further, he allowed a picture of his countenance to be taken at that time that she might realize the occurrence was more than a dream. (JW I was told by my teacher and Guru Merelle Fagot that Thedra had a large format camera called a 620, if I remember right, and it had bellows on it and founded out. She used this to take the picture of Sananda. Merele said that she got some real good pictures with that camera. I have seen this picture that Thedra took and Sananda didn't look very handsome, he just looked like a normal person with not too long of hair and he had very dark skin.) Sanada's Message to her by Sister Thedra.

"Sori Sori: Mine hand I have placed upon thine head, and I have given unto thee the authority to use Mine name. Give unto them the name Sananda, by which they shall know Me as the Lord thy God - the Son of God, sent that ye be made to know me, the One sent from out the inner temple that there be Light in the world of men." (The meaning of "Lord God: "The Lord God, for he is "Lord" of, and responsible for, that which he has brought forth.)

"Now it is come when ones which have the will to follow Me shall come to know Me by that name which I commanded thee to give unto the world as Mine "New name." There are many that shall call upon the name of Jesus, yet, they will deny the new name as they are want to do. While unto thee I give assurance that I am the One sent that there be Light in the world of men. Now let this be understood, that they that deny Mine New Name deny Me by any name. So be it I have appointed thee Mine spokesman; I've given unto thee the power and authority to speak for being that which I AM. And I say unto thee Mine child whom I have called forth and anointed thee with the Holy Spirit, thy name shall be as it is now called, Thedra - that name I spoke unto thee from out the ethers, and thou heard Me and accepted that which I gave unto thee; and wherein have I deceived thee? Wherein have I forgotten thee, or left thee alone?"

"I say unto thee, Mine hand is upon thee and I shall

sustain thee and you shall come to know that which I
have kept for thee. So be it that I have kept thy
reward, and at no time shall it be dissipated of
scattered, for it is intact. So let this Mine Word
suffice them which question thee - let them question,
and I shall bear witness for thee. For do I not know
  Mine servants from the traitor?
Do I not reward Mine servants according unto their
works or merits? I speak that they might know that I am
mindful of Mine servants, that I am not a poor puny
priest who has forgotten his servants."

"I say unto them, Mine servants shall be glorified
above the crowned heads of the nations which have set
themselves apart, and denied Me Mine part of Mine word
for they have turned from Me in their conceit and
forgetfulness."
"Now let this go on record as Mine Word, and I shall
give unto them proof, which are of a mind to follow Me.
So be it as I have spoken and I am not finished; I
shall speak again and again, and I shall rise Mine
Voice against them which set foot against Mine
servants, and they shall be as ones cast out. So let
them ask of Me and I shall enlighten them. So be it I
know where of I speak. Be ye as ones blest to accept Me
and know Me for that which I AM.
The Final Messages
On Saturday, June 13, 1992, at exactly 10.00 PM,
at the age of 92, Sister Thedra made her final transition from
the comfort of her own bed. When the time

arrived, she simply took one small breath and slipped quietly away, without pomp or fanfare.

She left as she had lived...as a humble servant for the greater good.

The messages that follow were given to Sister Thedra shortly before her transition.

They are compiled here to give you some idea of the significance of her passing and of the expansion of the work, as she is now free to work unencumbered by the physical limitations and by the pain which has so encumbered her in the past.

She has carried on the work here on the Earth plane for the last 50 years because that's where the work was needed...rest assured that her work now in the higher realms will simply be an extension of that work.

Sananda's Appearance

Be ye as one which hast heard Mine Voice and responded unto it - for I speak that ye hear, and I say that which is wise and prudent.

Let it be known that 1, the Lord thy God hast spoken and bear ye witness of Me, for I have made manifest Mineself that ye might know Me - and for this wast these manifestations made.

I say that I have made Mineself manifest that ye might see Me with thine mortal eyes; that ye might bear witness of Me. Yet thine companions saw and believed not; neither did they hear, for they were selfish and unprepared - yet, did I deny them?

I say; I came that they which would might see and hear. I went and came again unto Mine own. So be it that I have found; I have given unto the found that they which know not might know; that they might come to know as thou knowest.

Yet, how many hast turned from Me and persecuted thee for Mine Word. It is said, "Woe unto them which persecute Mine servants." is it not the law which they set into motion?

Yea Mine beloved, I say they bring about their own downfall. So be it that I am a compassionate one, and I would that they know what they do. So be it they shall learn well their lessons. So let it be, for this is the mercy of God, the One which hast sent Me.

So be it. I AM the Wayshower, the Lord thy God

I AM Sananda

PART I

Sori Sori: Mine word I have sent forth for the good of all -- yet not all shall take it unto themself. This is of their own choice -- each is given free will. None shall take that gift from them -- none shall trespass on another's gift of free will.

The time is come when there shall come from out the Cosmos a Voice which shall be heard throughout every corner of the planet -- and each shall hear it in his own language. He shall answer according unto his preparation, There shall be ones which shall hear and give no heed to it. Yet the ones which answer and give heed shall find their reward great, for I, the Lord God Sent of Mine Father, give unto them as I have received of Him.For this am I come this day as one of flesh and bone; Yea, I am come even as I promised so long ago.

Let it be understood that I am not limited to a body of flesh. I Am that I Am -- I am a Creator. I say I have created all form. I have given unto these forms life that they might move upon the planet, even as they were created to do. The creatures of the deep I've given life -- yea, the birds that fly -- the creatures that creep -- crawl -- I've said unto them "crawl -- ye are alive!"

Thus, I have gone out from Mine Father's House prepared to obey his command. He hast given unto Me the power and authority to create in His Name, even as He Creates. He hast given unto me the choice to create/ bring forth new forms, or to destroy the old and create a new -- for this I am watchful in that which is profitable to keep -- or to destroy. Be ye as ones to hear Mine declaration, for it is the word which shall not pass away. For that I say unto Mine servants which hear Mine Voice

1

and obey Mine mandate: Make ye record of these words that they be made known unto the generations to come. By the power of the spoken word, the mountains shall tremble, shake and shatter and be no more seen as mountains. The rivers shall run uphill and sink, leaving no place for man to set foot.

Now hear Me, ye child of Earth. I am speaking for the good of All mankind. Be ye not hasty to deny Mine word -- for have I not said, it passes not away? The word is power -- therefore I have said unto thee many times, watch thine tongue -- 'tis thy worst enemy. From out of thine own mouth shall come words which shall be cause of thine suffering -- or thine joy. While ye spew words of hate and condemnation, ye are creating for thine own torment.

Be ye as ones which can/will create anew -- that which shall deliver thee out of bondage -- free thee forevermore. This I would ask of thee for thine own sake -- lest ye be as one which hast betrayed thine own self. Know ye this: I am come unto this thine own planet, upon which ye abide at this moment -- yet ye shall be removed. Remember that ye are a guest of Mine, for I have prepared this habitat for thee -- I have planned well for Mine guests -- provided great store for thee.

What have ye given unto Me in return? Mockery -- scorn -- hypocrisy -- a poor penny which ye begrudge -- the foul words which is blasphemy -- which is a desecration in Mine sight?

O, Mine beloved creation, wherein have ye gone astray? Think ye not that I have forsaken thee for one moment! am One with thee -- I AM -- for that ye are One with Me. Consider that which I am giving unto thee -- then ye shall find that ye have chosen the better part which shall be thine eternal inheritance -- freedom from sorrow and shame.

Shame? Yea, shame is that which ye create by thine disobedience unto the Law which I have given unto thee, which is designed for thy total freedom -- that ye might enter into the Eternal Light.

* * * * *

Sori Sori: While it is yet time, let us consider the time. Time is of man's calculation -- Our time is calculated by events. It is now come when your present generation is ready for food that nourishes the Soul.

This nourishment I bring this day. These ones that I speak of may be six years or sixty--the years is of little count. The ones ready to partake of Mine portion are the ones which I shall feed. The ones which refuse Me and Mine gift, I shall pass by. Nevertheless, there shall be a place prepared for them -- they shall have their own place. Whatever they have made for themself shall not be denied them.

* * * * *

Sori Sori: This day we come as in concert with force (strength). We come that all might have the good news. This is the time of Great Action from the lowest to the highest of mounts. I say unto ye, We of the heights have stooped unto the lowlands which have given unto thee footing the eons of time. Now it is come when the call hast gone out, "COME HOME." Long have ye Mine children, wandered in the lowlands, knowing not from whence ye went out. Now it is come when many Great Ones from afar hast come unto the Call -- the cries of the ones just awakening.

O, could ye but know the love and mercy of these ones which have bent low to be unto thee Older Brother, that ye might find thy way back unto thine home, the place from whence ye went forth. That which is thine divine inheritance awaits thee. We call, "O wanderers in bondage, Come Home."

Let these calls which go forth from out the Cosmos fall softly upon thine ears -- for ye shall be as one to rejoice forevermore when ye heed the call and prepare thineself to come home with Us.

We have gone before thee to prepare the way before thee. We have kept thine fortune for thee -- know ye what that is? Nay, I say ye have forgotten thine inheritance, willed unto thee from thine time of going into bondage.

Let thine heart be softened -- thine ear quickened -- thine tongue be given unto praise. O, Mine beloved children, wherein hast thou found PEACE? -- wherein have ye found comfort from fear -- pain -- hatred -- injury -- and wherein have ye found wisdom?

Let it be understood that this is a New Day -- a day of awakening, when the laggard shall fluff off the laggardly cloak -- break the chains which hast bound him -- the sinners shall cry for forgiveness and mercy.

Yea, Mine precious children, ye shall come to know that which We say unto thee this day. That which was said in "olden times" was said for thine understanding in that time, as ye know time.

There are today -- within thine places of the world of man -- which heard the call in those days of yore, which betrayed themself. They are as ones walking the Earth this day, crying and pleading for freedom.

Yea, they shall be heard and answered, for none goes unnoticed. Yet it is said, ye shall do thine part -- the law is plainly written -- even

4

within thine heart it is written. Be ye alert and ye shall not fail, for there is a Great host which stands ready to give unto thee loving and gentle assistance when ye have cleansed thineself.

Let go all thine hatred -- gossip -- jealousy -- covetousness -- thine wars and whoredom. Give unto thine neighbor no pain -- take not his bread from him -- cause him no fear -- do unto him as ye would he do unto thee -- love him as ye love thine self. Have ye loved thine self as We love thee? Ponder these Mine words and answer truly -- dost thou love thine self? Give unto Me thine heart, thine hand, thine head -- sayeth the Lord God unto thee. Hear ye Him and heed that which is said unto thee this day.

* * * * *

Thedra: [my vision] I am stripping beds for laundering. All beds were empty -- no more sleepers.

* * * * *

Sori Sori: This is the day of action when the sleepers shall awaken and no longer shall their beds comfort them, for they shall up from them filled with the Spirit of inspiration. That which is within them shall come alive as a flame which shall no longer be quenched by the darkness. There shall be a Great Awakening, and the wonderment of it shall cause their hearts to leap for joy! They that awaken shall sing Great Paeans of Praise unto the Glory of the Father which hast given unto them Life -- so be it a Glad Day.

Rejoice that this day is come, for many have come from far galaxies that this might be accomplished. O Mine children, could ye but see that which is being done on your behalf -- how you would rejoice -- there would be no fear or slothfulness.

Give unto Me credit for knowing that which I say unto thee -- for I have the greater vision. I see from the heights wherein there is no cloud -- no tears -- no anguish. Joy abounds for every one which enters into Mine place of abode. So be it Amen.

* * * * *

Sori Sori: Much has come into manifestation since we began these letters -- yet ye are entering upon a new phase of this thine commission -- assignment, shall I say. Bless this day, for great shall the blessings flow as the gentle river which ye were shown.

This shall be as the New Day -- the new beginning wherein man shall arise from their lethargy -- the long aeons of sleep. The awakening is come. Happy shall be the ones which arise and come forth in the Light – that which shall be their freedom -- their resurrection from bondage.

Many which know not that they have been in bondage shall cry for joy and sing songs of praise unto the FatherMother God for their freedom. Let this be heard from every voice -- every living creature -- even unto the frog shall sing for joy!

The porpoise -- the whale -- the dolphin -- the flying creatures -- shall sing with angelic voices. Yea, every living creature shall be free and express such joy as man hast not known. O, glad shall be We of the Host, for long have we worked and watched for this holy day. Yea, a Holy Day shall it be -- for all the Host of Heaven have gathered for the occasion of this which shall be the Great Festival -- "Coming Home".

6

Many yet unborn shall take part in this, the greatest of all festivals. They shall be the Angel Band. Can ye imagine such a festival? 'Twill be remembered and celebrated throughout the Cosmos -- for many hast come from afar to prepare for this Great Day of rejoicing.

Give ye forth with praise and preparation. Prepare thy wedding garments, for the Bridegroom awaits thee. Put on the garment -- which fades not -- which grows more brilliant at the knowledge that ye are free. Ye could not look upon such an one arrayed thusly before ye are freed.

We have called long and loud, "Come Home, Come Home." We have touched thee and whispered softly while ye have slept, that ye be as ones prepared for the coming in. O, great shall be the joy -- even We of the Host tremble at the foresight. Yea, we do see that which is preparation -- even its finish. Give ye thanks, O Mine blessed ones, that at last ye shall find glorious peace forevermore. Hast it not been written of old that this day would come --- referred to as the "resurrection day" when the sleepers shall come out of their tomb - "grave"? Know ye the meaning of that -- the word so often mumbled from the edifices set aside for me? Do the ones which have thought themself enlightened know?

Nay, I come declaring unto all people -- the day of knowing -- thine understanding is upon thee. Look ye with eyes that see -- listen with ears that hear that which I say unto thee. Great shall be thy reward. Ye shall shake off thine shackles and arise from the grave in which ye have buried thineself. Look up, reach up, for the Light surrounds thee. I say unto thee, great shall be thine reward. Yet ye shall shake off thine shackles -- arise from the grave in which ye have buried thine self. Reach up for the Light -- the Light surrounds thee -- 'tis cause of thine being, for ye live and breathe -- pulsate within the Light. Hast it not been said many times, I Am the Light -- surely it be true! for I have said it.

Now it is upon thee this New Day of thine home coming. Wait no longer -- fear not -- ask that ye see/feel the Light -- the joy. See the unencumbered angels which companion thee. They are too numerous to count. Ask of them that ye may know them by name -- by touch -- and they shall draw nigh unto thee - yet they are awaiting recognition. Be ye thoughtful and respectful of them, for they know not the way of the sluggard. They are a patient lot. They are the servants of God -- the ones which praise Him for the privilege of serving mankind. Even as the rebellious grumble, and defile themself before this august body of "Servants," they wait thine preparation.

* * * * *

Sori Sori: Mine hand I placed upon thine head -- I have anointed thee with sweet oil -- I have given unto thee a precious gift which shall be shared with all which shall ask to receive it.

The time is now this day, when many shall reach out, asking for solace -- comfort -- these Mine words shall be made available unto them. For it is necessary that they find comfort in the days ahead, for great shall be their frustration and suffering.

The word I would have them take unto themself is that which I have promised unto All mankind when they are prepared to receive. These shall be brought out before the day of great sorrow which cometh ere there is another moon. I say unto one and all, Hear ye Me, and fear not, for I am Captain of this Ship, I know well Mine part.

Behold ye the heavens and give ye thanks that it is so. Have I not given unto thee the gift of Life? Have I not provided a place for thy foot? The Earth I hold within Mine hand -- She hast nurtured thee at Mine behest -- hast thou taken note?

Be ye thoughtful of thine Source -- thine Being. I say there are the slothful which know not -- neither do they care. They ask not for knowledge -- or blessings -- they go about blindly fearing for their "being" -- their family -- supply -- knowing not that I am the provender. They have not seen Mine storehouse from which all supply cometh!

Be it such that no one should want. It is said: As ye are prepared so shall ye receive, yet ye are prone to ask of man the puny penny. Wherein have ye asked of thine "Source" which hast prepared a great feast for thee? It is said that the table is set before thee. The call is gone forth, "COME, Come ye to the feast." Hast thou heard that call? Knowest the meaning thereof?

Let us speak of the days to come. There is the part reserved for the one which hast awakened -- put on the fresh new garment worthy of the guest at the feast -- "The Wedding Feast". I say it is the "Wedding Feast" that ye have waited long for. Yet while ye have followed the piper, danced unto his tunes, I have called unto thee, Come, come. Have ye heard Mine call? | ask again, HAVE YE HEARD MINE CALL?

Let it be heard and answered, and ye shall rejoice forevermore. Go ye not into the dens of the dragon, the harlots and thieves. Yea, the thieves shall rob thee of thine inheritance -- the joy which should be thine by divine inheritance. Listen! Listen unto me, ye lukewarm ones which make a mockery of Me -- Mine word. Ye have desecrated the name "Christian" -- "Christ-ianity". Ye have sold thy birthright for a

9

poor penny - yea, a counterfeit penny. The pity of it -- O ye foolish ones.

Lo, it is by the grace and mercy of Mine Father, that he hast sent me for to warn and provide thee a plan by which ye might come home with Me. Have I not said, "I shall go and prepare a place for thee"? Think ye I come to amuse or entertain? Have ye not made a mockery of Mine word? Have ye not spat on Mine word?

Think ye to escape such as shall be thine lot? I say unto these, yea, unto these guilty of such abomination: There is the results of each act, word, deed, like unto it -- none escape. Know ye what vibration is? The justice is meted out like unto that which is sent forth. Watch! Watch! Watch! See -- listen -- and come clean of hands -- fresh of spirit -- pure of heart -- yea, as a little child willing to learn of that which is given unto them from the realm of Light. Many await thy sincere call.

* * * * *

At this hour it is found one which awaits the word I would have written for the coming generation -- they which shall be separate and different from the warriors -- the traitors of this infamous day of abomination.

It is written that "they shall go to war no more" -- it is so. There shall be peace among Mine children, for it is so decreed. Let it be known this day that I am at the helm of this ship. I have given unto each a plan, a tablet upon which their name is written, and that tablet shall be opened and they shall find therein all they have done, created, or caused to be created.

* * * * *

10

[The Vision] I, Thedra, am in the house. This house sits at the foot of a low hill, surrounded by verdure, where a group of mischievous young boys hid at night to play their pranks.

They are peeking in the windows all around the house, and have entered through the door. I go from window to window - then I find that they had found easy entrance. Now my whole attention is turned to finding a way to bolt the door. I look about for a plank that will reach from side to side. Papa enters -- I know he knows something about these things.

I go to a nearby house where they work for themself as "self-employed". I ask if I can get a board for a bolt. They said they didn't have such. I looked about and saw one just the size I needed, standing on edge, it was not dressed, but will do. I said, "that is a poor cat house with just one single board." I got it.

It is now getting dawn -- Lighter -- the sleepers begin to stir. I am concentrating on bolting the door. Now, as I am still watching the mischief-makers, I see some scatter for cover. I cry out, "I see you -- I can identify you! I have a pistol and I can use it!" This was a surprise to the sleepy-eyed ones just arousing themselves. "I need help!" I cried I see one fellow along the hill fleeing detection in fear.

Much confusion in the house. I see a tall, powerful woman walking down the hall, her back to me. I cried to her, "Where are you going? I need you -- don't go from me!!" (I knew we had been monitored.)

Now came a man to see me -- he seated himself outside on the ground. I went out to see what he was about. I sized him up, a flimsy, fat, careless fellow. He introduced himself as "Mr. Marco", master of the boys school down the road. Oh, I thought, the Marco boys! He had come to offer his apology for his boys. His words at parting were, "They do get out of hand sometimes".

The Sentinel

* * * * *

Sori Sori: It is said, as one is prepared, so shall he receive. It is now time that the sleepers bestir themself and arise -- for the time grows ever shorter, it is so written that one shall first ask of Me and I shall add unto their need that which is necessary for the work at hand. Let them listen, for I am speaking -- yea, I speak with many voices -- yet one truth do I speak. That which I say today I shall remember tomorrow. I do not forget that which I have said -- neither do I not know thine needs.

Be ye blest this day to remember that which I have said and caused to be written, that ye forget not I am the provender of Mine flock.

* * * * *

Sori Sori: Let this be for the good of all that I speak unto thee, for have ye not been prepared for to receive of Me? So be it, I shall speak clearly and fearlessly. There are ones which are impatient for action. I ask, what does it profit a man to run when he falls and has to be carried? Best to first measure his strength and his footing -- his strength before he jumps, is it not?

Now, for the second time I say, be ye as one which hast the responsibility of warning them of the hasty decisions, for no man knows that which I have in mind for him. Let it be as it is written that there is a Plan which goes not astray. It is given unto Me to know every step of the way -- yet it is easier, safer when one goes the way I point -- I direct -- for have I not seen them fall by the way when they think themself self-sufficient? It is written no man stands alone -- know ye that which this means? I am the root -- thou art the branches thereof. I am the Cause of thine Being and thou art the created -- therefore I am the Master -- ye are the Servant. I Am the Cause of thine Being, and because I am, thou art. Thou art the manifestation of Me in flesh -- therefore ye are One with Me -- My hand and foot made manifest -- therefore thou art One with Me -- why rebel against Me? This is the cause of all thine woes and confusion.

* * * * *

Sori Sori: I speak this day for the good of all -- for I am the Source of Knowledge -- I am that which sustains thee -- therefore thou art One in Me -- with Me. Ye are as Mine hand and foot made flesh. I speak the word and ye become that which ye are in "reality". Ye drop the veil of bondage -- which hast blinded thee from thine "totality". Wherein hast thou seen thine self as thou art? Ye have forgotten thine inheritance -- thine Sonship. Now I call thee out from the sleepers as ones which have the will to awaken. Yet, ye shall devote thine energy unto Me and Mine work without one thought of rebellion -- lest ye give unto thineself the bitter cup.

Pity art they which betray themself -- they are the greatest of fools, for they think themself wise. Now it is come when I am calling loud and long from the four corners of the Earth: Arise from thine dreams -- thine beds -- wherein ye have slept overtime. Release the fables which hast comforted thee in thine delusive slumbers. Time now that ye listen for Mine voice and give serious attention unto that which I say unto thee, for it is said, and rightly so, that time as ye know it is short -- there

13

is no time for childish pranks or games. 'Tis, Mine little ones, serious time -- time for whole-hearted devotion unto thine calling. Fret not over little things, for I see the greater things which is [sic] to be done and with thine energy which shall be reserved for Mine work.

Now ye may say, Am I not doing thine work? | say unto thee: Ye know not that which ye are doing. Many are mocking Me -- Mine work -- Mine words. Ye know not which way ye should go; ye walk blindly, so to speak. Ye know not the meaning of Mine word, for ye are not as yet ready to hear Mine plan that I have been preparing for thee this day. Know ye that which I have kept for thee? Nay, ye have been bound by thine own preconceived ideas -- opinions -- while I have prepared the banquet for thine homecoming. Have ye seen Mine storehouse? Have ye seen Mine banquet which I have set for thine homecoming? Be ye blest to come unto Me. Ask of Me and I shall lead thee with surety and ye shall not fail!

* * * * *

Sori Sori: Let us speak of the Workers of Light. What think ye is meant by this expression, "Workers of Light"? I say unto thee it is one of the popular phrases among the people of your world of sleepers today. While they speak as the polly-parrot of the "New Age", they are yet asleep in their illusions. It is given unto Me to see them beat their drums and march to the bugler's tune. Yea, there are the marchers with their torches and banners, as proud of their banners. While I speak unto them of Mine banner, they have no comprehension of Mine meaning. I offer them the gift of freedom from fear and bondage -- what do they do? They say, "Yea, but what do I do -- what shall I do? I must do my part."

What say ye, Mine children? I ask of thee: What say ye? Can ye tell me ye have not heard Mine word? I have spoken unto thee by day and by night, even as ye slumber upon thy couch -- what do ye do? I see thee shake thine head in bewilderment and confusion. Ye run hither and yon -- for what do ye look? Give unto Me credit for knowing that which ye do -- that which ye need when ye are prepared for Mine instructions. Why art thou so restless -- do I not comfort thee? Do I not provide for thee? Ye may answer Me: "Yea, Lord, but"...but?"

I say for the many times, be ye at peace -- be ye still, silent of mind, and give ye credit where credit is due -- for I am the comforter -- the provender. I give and I take away -- I am the one which knows which is which, and what to give or what to take. Now be ye as ones which can ponder Mine sayings and it shall profit thee much, for I shall speak again and again. So be it and Selah.

* * * * *

While it is not yet time to give unto thee the full particulars of the Plan that our Brother has for thee, it is expedient that I add mine part or portion. There are those which we know as monitors which are at their post at this hour, that they might know what is best for thee. They give of themself selflessly. They are apt at their part, for long have they been at their post. It is given unto them to know that which is best for each and every one on the planet Earth -- they are creators. It is with the greatest love and wisdom that they keep watch o'er thee, for have they not brought thee hence?

I say unto thee, by their grace ye shall return unto thine Source of Being. I am but one of the host which hast come into thine field of comprehension. I find that many are wont to deny our existence. Others

15

see not the necessity to heed that which is given unto them, for they have not seen us -- neither heard our voice. While it is given unto us to be as ones knowing them as they are -- in totality -- we wait with patience -- while we see the word go out from their mouth and that which is created by it. Such is our wisdom -- expertise, shall we say!

While there are ones which have the comprehension of that which we are saying, they fear -- and "quake." So be it that we come into thine field of comprehension in clarity and for a purpose -- so be ye as one which can hold the Light for them which quake and fear.

The time of sifting and sorting is upon thee. It behooves every one which hast picked up the banner of truth and justice to step forth as a Light bearer unafraid -- steady of hand and foot -- clear of purpose. Yet some ask, for what purpose? Now I say unto them: For thine own sake, that ye be prepared for thine next phase. While we of the host know that, and that which it entails, there is the one which shall question, who are you? In whose name do you come? I shall speak unto that one -- be he female or male: I am one of the host sent in concert unto thine rescue. is that sufficient for this day? Know ye the meaning of mine words?

Let thine eye be single -- thine hand swift to do that which ye are directed to do -- and thine heart be fearless. For I say unto thee, when thine heart is pure -- thine hand is clean -- NOTHING of darkness shall touch thee. Not one thing of darkness shall enter into thine field -- neither shall it enter into thine house. Be ye as willing to learn, and for that shall we of the host enfold thee within our arms as a loving, caring parent -- for are we not? Behold the Light which we are. We are ever watchful -- protective -- for we are the "Gate-keepers". For this is our part we have at this "time" -- to protect them which have come from afar in the time so long ago -- forgotten by mortal mind -- the mission forgotten in the deep sleep which is now to be terminated.

That is why the clarion call hast been sounded -- Awaken! Awaken! Hast it been heard -- and by which ones? We observe them which have stirred -- these we are preparing grooming for the coming of the Bridegroom. It shall be a glorious day when we shall come together as One of Light - arrayed in Light. Thus we are -- and for that ye shall be spared

There be ones which ask: Spared from what? We say from bondage, which hast bound thee in darkness lo, many cycles which have come and gone. Which one would desire to repeat such bondage? Yet, we find there are ones which know not they are in bondage, for they are yet sleeping the sleep of the "dead". They know not that which they are -- neither from whence they came -- nor whither they goest.

Those are the ones which hear not the call -- these are the ones which deny our* existence. These, too, shall awaken -- even it be in another place -- another cycle -- for none are without mercy and direction -- it is freely offered. So be it and Selah.

I shall release Mine "pen" at this hour, that Mine servant might have her rest. Be ye blest to hear Mine message - for that hast it been penned for the good of all.

I AM -- thou art -- we are one in the Light of the One -- which is the Radiant One -- the perfect [symbol] - without blemish.

* the Host

* * * * *

17

Sori Sori: By Mine own hand shall ye be blest this day -- for this day do I speak unto thee. The time is at hand when there shall be great movement within the Earth. Many changes shall take place, and there shall be great sorrow and suffering. Yet it is said that them which hear Mine voice and obey it shall not be touched, it is given unto Me to be one which knows that which I am about. The things which I do are for the good of All -- yet I now speak unto the few which come into this place of Mine command -- Mine leading. Have I misled thee? Have I forsaken thee? Nay, I am at the helm of this ship. Know ye this, or are ye polly-parroting Mine words? Have ye seen Mine plan, even a small portion of it? Think ye that ye do that which ye do, ye do alone? This day I would ask thee, Ponder that which ye have done, and how have ye accomplished it? Ask ye of thine own self, how hast it come about? There are many which stand by to assist thee when ye are prepared to go forth with Mine plan.

Let me make for thee a parable. Know ye what a ball game is? Have ye played "football"? Are there rules? And are the players not in their right position? Just a thought to the wise. What of the well-trained soldier on the front lines? Do you get my thought? Good!

Let us proceed with the work at hand -- with understanding and trust -- for this do I speak this day. With these words I shall leave this portion. Be ye as ones prepared to follow Me where I lead thee.

* * * * *

Sori Sori: There are great plans afoot for this day. There are ones from afar which have come unto the place wherein I am, that they add their love and wisdom that the plan be brot to fulfillment in harmony.

18

Can ye say that ye are one with the ones which comprise the Host of Light? It is with great patience and love that we sit in Council while we see the children of Earth running hither and yon as a hill of misplaced ants. They look here -- they look there -- and ask of each other, what is this, what is that? Let us dissect this -- that we might find our Source. Ye have not found thine Source with all thine efforts -- thine learning.

It is now come when we of the host have drawn nigh unto thine beautiful planet upon which ye now abide -- that ye might come to know from whence ye came. Think ye that ye are that which ye call the flesh body of blood and bone? Ye shall be as one come alive -- then ye shall see thine true being as Light, wherein there is no darkness. Hast thou seen thine self as One with the cause of thy being? Hast thou been prepared to give unto Me thine hand, that I might lead thee through the night of thine deep sleep -- wherein are many pitfalls and delusions -- great suffering?

I ask of thee these questions, that ye might ponder upon them -- that ye might come to know what is meant by "reality". That which ye are in totality is One with thine Source of Being, as we of the Host see thee as whole -- perfect. Yet we see that which ye "think" thy self to be -- this is that which concerns us at this moment of your time. For it is expedient now that ye awaken from thy slumber and shake off the lethargy -- lest ye be as the sleeper still. It is given unto thee to think that ye are awake -- yet we know that which ye are in totality and that which ye think thine self to be.

There is no time when ye have not been under the observation of the Mighty Council -- which has the Plan, the MIGHTY PLAN within their hand. They follow thy path wherein ye stumble -- fall and cry out.

19

They pick thee up and place thee on firm ground, that ye mayhap grow stronger. Ye are admonished to look, see, and listen for the small voice within. Fear not, for I am the way, the Truth, and the Light.

Now, Mine beloved children, that the time is come that ones walk with thee from within the realms of Light, are ye prepared to walk with them? May it be so -- for this we speak in many ways -- many tongues, that ye may know that we are prepared to carry out the great and Grand Plan. We use many forms of communication, that none be without understanding of our existence. Yet we see thee -- the sleepers -- the unenlightened -- quibbling over the words, the language we use, for ye are so limited in thine own thinking, that we find many are so prone to think we are that which is limited.

Can ye see that which is thine totality -- the Cause of thine Being? Nay! Ye have as yet not glimpsed the previous sojourn upon this, thine place of abode. Ye are prone to seek out ones which are referred to as "Seers", which can tell thee these "secrets" -- are ye not? Sad, is it not? For we see not in part -- as ye do. We are at the place in your so-called time when we see the fragment floating in a great sea of Light coming together within the center, the "Core" of all Light. Mine blessed children, what a blessed sight to behold!

Our purpose is to awaken the fragments unto that which is the whole of Being -- that there be harmony and joy. All fear and discord is of darkness -- unknowing -- which is darkness. We of the host are prepared to assist thee in thine awakening. For this are we making ourself known -- that ye may not suffer more. Why suffer more? Why art thou so prone to rebellion -- one against the other -- even against us, the Host? Ye even adopt ways to bargain with the ☉, the All, which we

20

are. We work in unison and as of one mind -- one purpose. can ye say as much?

Let us define our purpose -- for this do we make known the "purpose". The plan follows as ye are prepared to receive it -- in parts, shall we say. The purpose is to bring the Child of Earth Home -- in their pristine beauty, for nothing of darkness enters into our abode. Light and darkness cannot mix -- ne'er shall it. That is the purpose of our call -- that ye might awaken unto our touch -- our song, which we are singing throughout the Cosmos.

As each one returns unto his rightful home -- his place of going out -- the glad anthem shall be heard throughout the Cosmos, "Welcome Home! Welcome unto the Victor." This is the day so long awaited -- what joy shall be thine! We, the Host, shall be the host unto all which hast returned. So be it as the Father Wills it -- Let it Be.

* * * * *

Sori Sori: Behold the new dawn, for it cometh swiftly and with a loud shout. I say, behold the Glory of the New Dawn, for it is come! I am come with a mighty sword -- which shall cut away all the effluvia. So shall it be, so shall it be, for it is foretold of old there shall go forth great shouts of joy thru the Cosmos; Hallelujah! IT IS COME! IT IS COME! There hast gathered from the four corners of the Universe the Brothers of Light that they be present at the wedding feast when the Sons of God gather to greet the Bridegroom. "Hail! Hail! Hail to the Bridegroom" shall be heard as a great shout throughout all the Cosmos.

There shall be great Light flood the Earth, and she shall bring forth a generation of Sons which shall do her honor. And there shall be no

21

more war -- hatred -- malice -- jealousy -- and there shall be a New Moon. There shall be new fields within the Cosmos for the Sons of God which glorify the Father-Mother God. These fields shall be as nothing man can image. I say, as nothing man can image, for they shall be of purity -- purity -- and there shall be no taint upon the Sons of God therein. There are beauties unimaged by mortal man, for it is not yet come that he enter into the realm of purity -- such as cannot be spoken or penned.

It is now come that man hast begun to stir -- this is that for which we of the host come for to do. Be ye blest this day, for there shall come one unto thee which shall give unto thee great assistance, that ye might fulfill thine mission in the place wherein ye are. Know ye that we are aware of that which ye do and how it is done. So be it, we lend our hand and give assistance when expedient. We give no false promises or flattery, for that is not becoming unto us.

Let this be Mine word unto thee at this hour. Blest are they which hear that which I say. I Am the One Sent that there be Light.

* * * * *

Sori Sori: It is said that I am the Doorkeeper -- it is so. There are ones which think to bypass Me. I Am the Gate through which they -- one and all -- pass into the place wherein the Father abides. I Am the door of entry unto his Throne of Grace and Mercy. By His Grace I am speaking. By His Grace hast He sent me that ye might be brought back unto the place from which ye went forth.

They which hear Mine CALL and answer it -- then listen for Mine instruction and follow it -- which is the Law -- shall be as the "Prodigal

22

Son" returned. Can ye image what a glorious day that shall be? I say unto thee, there shall be ten thousand to sing Glory -- Glory -- Glory! A Son hast returned!!!

For this have we of the Host drawn nigh unto the little planet of Earth. We hear her cry -- she is in labor. The birth pains are as ye cannot hear, for thine inner ear is not open as ours, the Hosts. We have come unto the place of our headquarters, you would say, for the purpose of setting up a training station wherein ye, the ones which answer Mine Call, might be groomed -- prepared for the final day of preparation. Graduation would be a familiar expression -- one ye could understand. Therefrom, we shall take the novice for a greater initiation. When he hast finished that next part or portion of his learning, he goes into a place which is prepared for him, as he hast proven himself worthy and well prepared to add his part or gifts unto ours.

Now we have placed thee upon firm ground, ye shall be as one responsible for thine own part -- that of obedience unto the Word and giving credit unto us, the Host of Light, for thine directions. There shall be no rebellion, nor selfishness, for we shall be of one mind -- one purpose -- that of bringing thee out of bondage.

So let it be. Amen, Amen, and Amen.

* * * * *

Sori Sori: Be ye blest by me. As Mine own hand shall ye pen the contents of this book, which shall go forth as Mine word unto each and every one which seek the Light which I Am. There are ones which look for Me in the sky -- others look for Me in strange far-off places -- while I am nearer than hand or foot. It is with the Love of Mine Father which

23

hast All Power, that I now speak unto the child which is upon the planet Earth, bound by opinions and preconceived ideas. He/she is the one which this message is designed for.

While it is the intention of the Great and Mighty Council to monitor each and every person upon the planet, there shall be no mistakes, for our monitoring system is quite sufficient. Ye have not as yet envisioned our efficiency. By the Great and Grand Council shall thy record be kept. Accurate shall they be, for We work within the Law of the Cosmos. We know that which goes on within the halls of your learning. We know that which goes on within the pits of darkness. Think ye that ye are wise? I say unto thee, ye are in darkness.

For this have We set about to bring thee home -- the place from whence ye went forth so long ago -- times beyond thine comprehension. Have ye remembered thine going out from the Father's place of abode as one pure? Pristine pure thou were. Ye have gone out as ones fearful and self-conscious. Ye have wandered and wondered -- asking of others in darkness and bondage, "Who am I? Why am I here? Where did I come from? Where will I go when I die?"

These are the things I shall address within this little book. With Mine own hand I shall cause it to be brought forth -- for the good of All which seek freedom from bondage and the return unto their rightful estate from which they-ye have gone out. Be ye blest, each and every one which shall accept Mine humble offering as a precious gift.

* * * * *

Sori Sori: Be ye blest this day -- for this have come. This is Mine time to give unto this part which shall be added unto Mine book, which shall

24

be called, "The Book of Sananda," which shall be for to awaken them which sleepeth yet.

There are the ones which hast begun to stir -- these are the ones which shall seek me out. These are the ones which I shall touch, and they shall come alive and do that which I shall give unto them to do. These shall be blest for that which they shall do.

There shall be a great stirring within this generation which is now in flesh, for the time is now at hand. There is a great cry heard which goes out into the Cosmos -- it is heard and it shall be answered. This cry is one of the heart. Therefore, many have gathered in the place which hast been prepared as the new training center in which these shall be brought and trained as they are prepared. There shall be many from the realms of Light which are prepared to groom them for the next place wherein they shall go for greater or higher learning.

Now, let it be understood I am speaking unto these ones which shall open their eyes -- their ears -- their heart unto the call which hast gone out -- for none are brought in against their own will. This is the law that ye seek Me out. For I am the Light -- I am the door through which they enter. They shall have their passport which shall be in order, for there are none which enter without. They shall be as ones fully prepared to go all the way with Me -- and they shall find that they have chosen wisely.

For I am the One sent that this new order be established for the good of All. Let it be recorded for the record of them which shall read these Mine words herein, that this New Order shall be as none before, for the old order hast now this day become defunct. It no longer shall hold the children which are born unto the Light-bound, for there shall be sent abroad in the land the great wave of Light foretold in these Mine messages. There shall go with that a Great Light-wave - a Great Sound -- a trumpet, shall I say. This trumpet shall be as none other which ye have known, for it shall echo throughout the land. It shall awaken the sleepers. They shall arise from their beds of lethargy and answer the call: Come! Come! Come all ye that have heard Mine call and rejoice with Me that this day is come -- that ye have heard and answered.

By Mine own hand shall I bless them which are prepared. For this are We of the Host prepared to welcome them into this place of learning for which We have worked diligently -- for long have We labored. This is Our gift of love unto each and every one which shall be prepared to enter into this place, which shall be the place in which they shall be brought for the next part of their training which shall prepare them for the greater learning.

From this place or school, they shall go with another passport in hand which shall admit them. Be ye assured that ye shall be as one which shall know that which ye have done to earn that passport, for there is no guesswork -- nor cheating within this place which I am speaking of. These which go forth with their passport shall know that which they are to do, for they are prepared for a "new part". They are as ones filled with joy and anticipation. They are brave -- of courage -- staunch and pure of heart -- ready to stand in the Light of the Radiant One. They shall stand as the Lighted ones which have earned their passports.

Be it so, that there shall be many which await this day of their entrance into this new place of which I speak. Let it be a glad day, for there are ones which walk amongst thee of flesh and blood which are thy Benefactors -- thine Guardians, that ye might not fall -- that ye be

26

prepared for to enter into this New Place, wherein ye shall be taken by one of these enlightened guardians/benefactors. These, thy devoted brothers, have walked the same path, which they know so well. Therefore, they are well prepared for that part. They have chosen their part solely for their love of these who are the sibets. There shall be serenity and fellowship. Each shall be known unto the other, for they shall be of one mind -- of one purpose.

Let it be known that I, Sananda, shall be the Head of this training center, and it shall not be aborted. It is said: "Not a plan goes astray -- only Mine sheep." This is the day of sifting and sorting. The sheep shall not enter into this, the New Place, for this is a training school, shall I say, wherein the Shepherds shall be prepared for a new part or portion.

Blest art they which are prepared to enter therein.

* * * * *

Sori Sori: Let us continue with our subject -- the School which is now in progress. When one is now prepared to enter into this place (and be ye assured it is "A Place"), they shall be appraised of it and we shall bring them in with assurance that they are in good hands. For this is a place in which there is Love as man hast never known -- Light as he can bear. For the Seniors know their capacity and their intent -- their dedication. For this shall We see that they are cared for and prepared for the next step of their preparation, which shall be their enLightenment -- even greater. This is the day of EnLightenment, when the ones so prepared shall know that which he came for to do. He shall take up his Light and go into his next assignment as one with great assurance and forbearance.

There shall be with him a monitor and a teacher which hast been well prepared to reveal the precepts and truth unto him. He shall carry with him his true identity, and his passport shall be in order. There shall be no distractions -- none to place a hand upon him which shall turn him away -- or to distract his attention. He shall be whole-hearted in his study; fully devoted shall he be -- for this shall he be called, as We know well his capacity/ his intent. By the Grace of the Father-Mother Eternal shall they go forth in the Eternal Light which directs them, which naught of darkness shall touch.

Now, it is come when there shall be gathered together for the purpose of caretakers of these which are to be the ones which have answered the call. These ones shall bear the Seal of Melchizedek, and upon their forehead shall be written a new name. They shall know that name as the Seal -- which shall be seen and recognized by each and every one of the Host, which shall be as their brothers and sisters which have been through this School. They know every step of the way in which these ones which are now entering upon their initiation, which shall be their entrance unto the greater learning. When this is accomplished, there shall be a great cry of joy and a great feast, such as none hast imaged. What a glorious day it shall be for each one which hast given of himself that there "Be Light" -- Light, which shall be shared with All mankind without thought of self.

Sananda shall be Head Master, and all shall know Him as He is. Great shall be the joy of them which are gathered within this place which is now prepared. So be it and Selah.

* * * * *

Sori Sori: The time is at hand when there shall be a gathering in of the ones prepared to enter into this place wherein We have come and prepared for them which shall be brought in. There are the ones which have proven themself worthy -- which have followed the precepts and commandments of this Order, of which I am the Head. Now, when the last one hast been brought in, there shall be a portion which shall be released unto the remaining company which was not prepared to enter this place.

Now, let it be said, this portion given unto them which have not entered this place shall have the lesser portion -- for they have not the strength of character to enter into this "School". I say "School": This is a training school as the ones which are yet in the outer school has not dreamed of. Yet they which are in the outer school shall go through a swift and mighty training in a very short while of Earth time.

It hast been said many times, "Time is short -- be ye up and about the Father's business." While many have laughed at the "workers of Light" -- have ye not heard it? have ye not seen it? These which laugh and mock shall cry out, for they shall find they have chosen the poor part. Give unto Me credit for being that which I Am. There are none which shall call Me a liar and a rogue.

There is now a weighing, a balancing, a sifting and sorting -- which shall be for the great harvest which is now being brought in. This is told unto thee in the Book of Old which ye cherish as Truth. Ye shall find therein many things ye have not understood -- the language mayhaps be different -- the message the same -- and sufficing. Few understand that which I am saying this day. Hast thou heard what I have said -- or have ye ridiculed Mine chosen, which hast been Mine hand made manifest that ye have that which hast been written, that ye be prepared for this day of deliverance? Yea, this <u>IS</u> the day long foretold.

Where do I find thee this day? In what place hast thou dwelt? Hast thou made thine bed one of blessed rest, or one of shame and sorrow? Hast thou given of thine self to one which hast brought shame and suffering? Hast thou given of thine self that some forgotten, starving child be comforted, fed and clothed and loved? Pray ye for them which cry out in pain and suffer for the love of a parent which has lost a child -- knowing not that there is no death. Have ye comforted the sick, the dying. Hast thine heart been pure in that which ye have taught thine children -- thy wards -- what of them? Have ye nourished -- nurtured them as thine own? Blest art they which can answer, "Yea, Lord, I have."

This I would ask of thee, hast thou destroyed one of Mine little ones which had not the time to breathe the breath of life? I say unto thee, there shall come a time when ye shall see that one so aborted face to face. Ye think, "It is done -- finished." Nay! Nay! Not so! for ye have not reckoned with the <u>Law of Life</u>. O ye physicians, Awake! Awake! Learn the great lessons of life. Think ye wise? Wherein have ye been schooled? The pity of it! We see thee as ones moving amongst a great, black horde of entities which overshadow thee in thy dark deeds.

I say ye are in the pit -- the darkness which consumes thine being. There is no Light from or within the places wherein the practices of death are common and of the darkness. There's a huge black cloud of despair which hangs about these places of abortion. Yea, the huge crowds which cry for their <u>freedom</u> to <u>abort</u> -- what of them? ye may ask. They know not that which they do -- the pity of it. They are within the grasp of the greatest of traitors -- the one which brings death and

30

sorrow unto these kind which are willingly following him. He is the prince of darkness. ! hear them say, Who's that? -- with a sneer go their willful way. Sorrow follows them -- it is the law. Behold ye the law at work. See the hand of God -- the cause of thine being, move -- it is sure and swift! Behold ye the day of reckoning -- for it comes swiftly.

* * * * *

Sori Sori: This I would have thee say unto the true seeker of Light: He need not wander in darkness to find it -- for Light and darkness do not mix. There is no darkness within the Light which I Am. The seeker which goes from house to house inquiring of Me shall not find Me in any of these, for I am not housed in any building. I need no bed-pillow for my head. I am free of all bondage -- all portions which hast bound thee.

Now it is come when I say again and again, I am of Mine Father Sent. He hast given Me mine authority to bring thee Home -- the place from which ye went forth in the beginning. He hast given Me the power and authority to create as He creates. We are One -- One, even as ye are One with Me. There is no division -- no separation -- only within thy world of illusion.

Ye shall now seek the Light which is thine Source of Being. Therein is no sorrow -- no darkness. This is that I would have for thee, Mine children which cry out in terror of the darkness from which all thine pain and sorrow. Let it be understood that I am with thee, closer than hand or foot -- for I am the cause of thine being -- thine Eternal Being. I am thine Breath -- for this do I say we are One. Ye see thineself as separate -- yet ye are under the veil of illusion.

31

I am come unto thee as thineself made flesh. I animate thine body of flesh -- which ye call "me-mineself." I tell thee, ye are Spirit -- incarnate. I say I give unto the body of flesh Spirit of Mine Spirit. And ye breathe in my portion which is Light -- Life of Mine Life I give unto thee. Mine life flows even as a gentle breeze -- in and out -- in and out -- back, and back again -- ever pulsating. In waves does it come -- flow as life of Mine life. Ye are held by Mine pulse, for we beat with rhythm for there is nothing save Light -- "It" is All. All else that ye perceive to be real is illusion, which shall pass away as naught.

Now it is come when ye, Mine children of the Light, shall awaken. I say unto thee, ye shall come to know Me -- yea, better than that which ye <u>think</u> thineself to be. For this have I made myself flesh, that ye might have comprehension of that which is real and the power of Light -- Spirit. Give unto thine self credit for being a child of Light -- for this art thou immortal -- eternal. There is no death. That which ye perceive as death is but the ebb and flow of the mighty waters of Spirit/Light!

Behold ye that which shall be shown unto thee -- for We of the Realm of Reality, known as the Illumined Ones, are preparing a "School" in which ye shall learn first-hand that which cannot be conveyed by pen or voice. Therein ye shall see and know as I know. Therein ye, the ones which are prepared to enter this place, shall see and learn and know that which shall be <u>revealed</u> through sight -- and sound, as ye now know nothing of -- for the tones are not yet heard by man of flesh.

* * * * *

Sori Sori: This is Mine word unto thee at this hour: There are none which know the fullness of Mine plan. Yet ye shall be as ones which have parts in it, for without one My plan could not be perfect or completed. It is said, and rightly so, that it -- The Plan -- shall not fail. For this have I been sent of Mine Father -- for He hast given unto Me the authority to go forth as His hand and foot made flesh upon the Earth.

Now it is come when I shall gather together Mine flock and give unto them that which is needful for their preparation to return unto Him with Me -- for none can enter into His place of abode unprepared. This I would have thee understand: I am the One Sent that ye be prepared. There are none which enter into His abode save through Me -- for I am the Doorkeeper.

There are parts for every one which follows Me. Each shall have his place, his seat, and his part. None shall be out of place -- neither shall he be left alone. There are many which shall be unto him which enter, fellows -- which have gone before him to give unto him that which is necessary for his "initiation" into the place wherein he shall go. These ye may speak of as Angels -- yet ye know not that which they are or that which their position is. For ye which hast not yet seen or experienced cannot image such purity and splendor -- for thine eyes could not behold them in their glory!

It is written that there shall be a great Light flood the Earth -- it is so. This is the day of revelation and fulfillment of the Holy Writ. Be ye not deceived by the world of darkness and illusion. For this have I been sent into the world -- that all men be brought out. Yet there art many which do not think to receive Me or the freedom I bring -- the gift of freedom so precious -- the gift of their inheritance in full -- given of the Father, the Source of thine Being. Many there be which shall give unto Me the bitter cup. Yet they shall drink of it, for it is the law they shall drink of the cup which they have prepared for another -- be it sweet or bitter.

This day is the day for which man of Earth hast waited. While he hast thought it to be far distant and of little concern unto him, he hast deluded himself while he hast ran to and fro, looking backwards, searching for his Source, looking for his heritage, his "roots". I might ask, What hast he found? What hast he learned from all his labors? Hast he found peace -- freedom? His lineage he knows not -- his work hast availed him naught!

Now -- this day - I come fully prepared to reveal his Source, his place of abode, his rightful estate unto him that he might have eternal life -- no more bondage -- no more suffering -- no more sorrow. What do I find? I find him -- man of Earth -- sleeping and eating -- drinking -- dancing -- making merry and thinking himself wise, while it is now upon him that which shall bring him "up short" when he is face to face with that which is now come to pass. He shall find that which he hast feared is now upon him. There shall be much unrest, suffering and confusion. Yet I tell thee, ye shall not escape that which ye have sown -- be it "wheat or tares" -- it is the law.

"Man" is the whole of mankind. We of the Light see the whole -- too, We see each one as a living soul. Each hast his own Light, which hast its number. Its code, its number is encoded within the Light of the soul -- which is revealed unto Us of the Light which comprise the "Hierarchy" which are not of Earth. Yet they are the ones referred to as the "White Brothers", while that is not always understood. What is meant by the "White Brothers"? Many claim to be one of this company -- while they are but revealing their foolishness, for their boastings find them out.

Be ye not deceived, Mine beloved ones. I come unto thee as one of Light -- Light I AM. I speak unto thee in parables -- that which ye can understand. I come not to confuse -- or make flowery preachments. I come that ye might learn of Me and the Host which I bring with Me. These are the ones which have won their "Victory". I have spoken unto thee of the "Victor", which is he that hast won his freedom from bondage by his own effort and application unto the Law which is just and merciful. As he hast sown so shall he reap.

I speak simply, that all might hear/comprehend that which I say or mean. Let them which have an ear to hear -- hear that which I say, for there are none which rebel against Me shall enter into the place wherein I am -- wherein they shall find sweet Peace and eternal freedom.

Let these Mine words be added unto that which I have caused to be recorded -- and ye, Mine hand made manifest, shall rest thine physical body for this hour.

* * * * *

Sori Sori: Be ye blest this day for thine service to Mine children in bondage. I have told thee of a School which is now established wherein ones shall go for to learn of the Light and the "Light Workers" and what they do -- and what their mode of instruction is or shall be. Now this School shall be as none other, for it shall be as a place within the near Earth, while not upon it. It shall be for the ones which are prepared/willing to go all the way with Me, for I am the Head of this plan. The precepts are not new at all. Yet there are many which have not, lo these many cycles, have not bothered to learn what these precepts is (sic) -- what it entails. There are and have been ones among the Eartheans which have taught these principles. Some have known

35

them well. Even so, they have failed their passport; their passage aborted.

Now it is come when there's a new dispensation and expediency -- which hast been met by the Love and Mercy of the "Sons of God" which have volunteered for their assignment -- that of coming from afar to establish and maintain this School which shall be established within the first sector of the atmosphere of the Earth. This shall be as a private/secret place -- where none shall approach without passport. No scientist shall find or approach it by his own will or effort, for in that place there shall be great and wonderful things revealed and they shall be very carefully guarded wherein no man shall pilfer or trespass.

* * * * *

Sori Sori: There are ones now prepared to enter into this School which shall be as none other. The part which shall be as the receiving station shall be near unto the Earth, wherein there shall be Light and love. The candidates shall be brought in from the north, south, east and west -- as they are prepared. None need be appraised of their destination or that which they are to do -- yet they shall have no fear. They shall have full trust and patience. They ask not for proof, for they are as ones prepared to follow where I lead. By Mine own hand they shall be led. They shall know Me as I know them.

I am the Shepherd which knows Mine sheep. They shall be fit and prepared to do that which is assigned unto them. For this shall they give their full attention -- their loyalty and support unto the Order which is the Order of Melchizedek -- be it the Order of the Cross and Crown. None shall find their way alone. Those which think to bypass Me shall find that they are the traitor unto themself -- for I am the door thru

36

which they enter. Now that ye have been appraised of this, ye shall stand up and be counted -- for it is said ye shall be as ones called/numbered, and thy name shall be written in thy forehead. Thy name shall be as none ye have been given by any Earthean, for it shall be that which is encoded within thine hand.

Before ye shall enter, one shall come unto thee and touch thee. Ye shall be as one receptive of His touch, for it shall carry with it vibrant tones as nothing known before, Now I shall give unto thee a key which ye shall hold within thine heart where none other might pilfer it -- for it shall be thine own and shall serve thee well when it is called for. Now, ye shall not speak of this key, for it is thine and thine alone. Ye shall humbly receive it -- humbly keep it as thine own, for none other could use it.

When it is come, ye shall leave behind everything! There shall be nothing taken with thee. Ye shall come as thou art -- empty-handed -- for there shall be no need of any of thine possessions -- for "We" are not impoverished. Be ye as one which can come as ye are. Lay down all thine preconceived ideas and plans, for ye know not that which We of the Host have in store for thee.

I have spoken of the "Plan" which no man knows, for it is conceived and brought forth by the "Christ Council". All thine learning shall avail thee naught, for it shall be as new- and yet, not strange unto thee for ye shall have this new part so imprinted within thine memory that ye shall have it restored unto thee. Then ye shall cry out for joy and be glad that ye have endured unto this day of awakening. It is a straight and narrow path that ye have chosen -- yet worth all the trials and suffering.

Ye shall honor thine teachers, mentors, "guides", and fellow brothers which have held thine hand when the path was steep and dangerous. They have given unto thee comfort when ye have been in need -- they have given succor in the time of sickness and uncertainty. Let thine mind be stilled -- thine heart be pure -- thine hands clean -- thine footsteps firm and sure. Then ye shall be sure of the touch. Thine number shall be called for (or because of thine preparedness.

* * * * *

Sori Sori: By the grace of the Brothers of the Council shall ye be brought in, and ye shall not want; therefore, ye shall come as one unencumbered. This is Mine instruction unto the uninitiated -- this should be sufficient instruction at this time. Weary not of thine waiting, for I assure thee it shall be very profitable unto thee.

* * * * *

Sori Sori: Let us speak of the Council which is in preparation of the said School, that ye which are prepared to enter might know more of us which make up this Council. These which are the Council are known as the Father's right hand. They are His hands and feet made manifest within the Cosmic realms. They comprise the Angelic force, the Eloheim, the Creators of the Light realm. They are the Guardians of the planetary systems, the populators thereon. They are the ones which hold within their hand the Plan which no man knows. They have the power and authority to give and take -- for they have all power which is given unto them of the Father of All -- the one which is the Cause of BEING -- all that He Is. Nothing exists save Him. He is without form or limitation of any kind. He is the ALL -- the beginning and end -- the Alpha and Omega.

Therein We of the Christ exist as one with the All. We are as one mind -- one body -- comprised of the many which is the power and action of the Father. It is for this unity and wisdom, motivated by His Love, that holds the Universes in orbit -- which causes the worlds to be populated with the great diversity of beings, which are the ones that ye know not of. Ye shall come to know that which hast been hidden from thee, for ye have gone out into fields afar and wandered in darkness and despair -- forgotten thine place of going out. Now it is come when thine number shall be called, and ye shall answer and return unto thine rightful estate.

For this are We of the Council sending ones unto the Earth to rescue the ones which are prepared to enter into this place We have prepared to bring them to/into for greater learning. This shall be the place of preparation or grooming for the next phase of thy learning, which entitles thee unto. greater, more glorious revelation/understanding of the Cosmos, wherein ye shall learn that there is no limitation -- only Love, Light and Oneness.

I AM -- for that ye art -- so be it and Selah.

* * * * *

Sori Sori: This day ye shall give unto Me the hand which shall hold the pen, and we shall do that which is expedient. The hour swiftly approaches when there shall be a great wave of sound which shall reverberate around the Earth -- it shall rock and roll. There shall be ones which shall run and hide their faces, while there shall be no escape from this experience -- which shall be well, for it is foretold that there shall be a great awakening. It is said none shall escape, for this is the day long foretold and recorded in thine holy books of old.

I say unto thee this day, be ye prepared for that which shall come upon thee. Now it is come when ye are offered thy salvation -- hast thou heard "that" before? And what hast thou done? Be ye sober and ponder Mine words, for I come as thy deliverer. Fear naught. Be ye as one which can hear and comprehend that which is given unto thee -- for thine own sake do we reveal this/ these things unto thee. Ye have been given bits and pieces, portions -- What have ye done with them? Have ye denied one portion and clung unto another?

I say unto one and all, be ye about thine preparation. Hear that which is said unto thee -- then be ye as one prudent, without judgment. Test thine source -- ask of the Source of thine Being, be this true? Then give unto thineself credit for comprehension -- without fear or self-judgment.

Now it is come when every one shall stand up and be counted. It is now come when the Great and Mighty Council has a plan that is so designed to fit the situation which now exists upon thy planet at this hour. It is said that there is a School now prepared for to receive them which have come out of their slumbers and declared themself ready to be received in this which I am speaking of. Have ye declared thine intentions? Have ye stood steadfast against the darkness -- the storms of temptation? How do ye stand this day? Are ye prone to say, I am ready, Lord? Are ye to give lip service and know not that which it means -- or the meaning of thine words? Art thou polly-parroting another's work? Have ye pilfered another's sayings to suit thine own situation -- to justify thyself?

These things I would have thee answer -- then say "Yea." Be ye not self-deluded, for ye shall read thine own record 'ere ye enter into this place which I have spoken of -- which shall be as a secret place unto the unprepared, for they shall not enter therein. Be ye not quick to ask or question -- where -- when -- and how do I get there -- where do I find this place of learning. For I say again ye shall first prepare thine own self by obeying the law (do not say ye have not been given the law), for it hast been placed before thee. Ye have but to look -- ask -- see -- it is not hidden!

* * * * *

Sori Sori: With these words I shall bring them into the place wherein they shall see Me -- for there are ones which have not seen Me -- neither have they heard Me. This I would have them know -- that I am within flesh and bone -- while flesh does not bind Me. I am free to go and come at will, for I have received Mine inheritance in full. I can be in any place I will at any time. No walls keep me out -- yet! am not an imposter -- neither do I go where I am not invited -- I know Mine way around! Be ye not deceived, for many claim to be Me -- this one which I Am. Ye shall know Me as I am when ye are prepared. Many make false claims.

While ye shall be as ones alert, for ye may be caught off-guard, there is that which is known as comprehension -- know ye what that is? 'Tis a gift of the Father. Ask for comprehension and look, see, and be ye not quick to ask to see the nail prints. For to them which ask I shall give no proof -- for ye shall be as ones which hast asked for comprehension and received as a Sacred Gift. For there are none so stupid as to forget their Benefactors -- lo, even to the Elementals which work with the soil are grateful for their part. Bless them, for they are part of the whole. Why art ye, which run to and fro, so blind? Ye see not the beauty about thee. Have ye stopped to smell the violet, the rose, the heliotrope -- to touch the willow -- the pine -- the ash which shades thee from the sun? Have the growing things not comforted thee -- given unto thee peace and joy? Wherein do you think these come from? How think ye they came unto thee?

Bless the Source, and be ye as one with it -- for it is thine beginning and thine end -- the Alpha and Omega which I Am. There is the Power and the Joy -- not the pretense of the ceremony which is so often shown at thine tables for the eyes of their fellow man. Give ye some thought -- pretense versus that which is within thine heart. Let it be from thine heart that ye say, "Thanks, Father."

Who is Father? Where is Father? What is His part? Dost thou know? Or do ye but make mock of Him? From Him all blessings come -- yea, from which thou hast thine Be-ing. Ye are One within the folds of His garment -- Light - - there is naught else. By Mine own hand have I blest thee, for I and the Father are One -- Is One.

* * * * *

Let us speak of the time spent in eating and drinking with little thought of the blessings -- from whence they come. Are they satisfied when they eat and run, or do they become bloated and feverish, sending out strange and uncomfortable sounds? Do they eat to nourish the body and soul?

Wherein have they found comfort and joy? Let them which forget from whence their blessing, take heed and send forth the thought of ones which have naught -- the hungry and dying of starvation. Ponder these things which I say unto thee -- for I have said there are none so stupid as the one which forgets his Benefactors. So be it and Selah.

* * * * *

42

Sori Sori: Wherein have they been fed and housed and clothed? Have they considered their Source? Have they given thought unto that which hast given unto them life? By Mine own hand hast they, one and all, been sustained. For this have We watched and provided for the children of Our creation. What have they to give unto Us of the Cosmos -- recognition?

It is now come when they shall be brought in and placed in the place prepared for them, for they have created that which they have created in the time of unknowing -- their slumber. They shall awaken! and come alive and know illusion to be false -- of their own creation. Then they shall lay down their burdens which they have carried through many a cycle. They shall arise as ones freed by their own choice and come forth with a great shout of joy!

Mine house is for the ones which have come for to learn of Me, and these shall apply themself unto their preparation, that they enter into this School which I am now preparing for to receive them. This is no small task, for it is an ongoing work -- We of the Host hast long been at this project. Have ye learned that which We have given unto thee in the time past for thine edification or preparation for this day? Nay -- not the many which have danced to the piper's tune. Let them now follow Mine call which shall sound throughout the land: Come! Come! Come follow ye Me! These ones shall know and be glad they have heard.

This I would say unto them at this time -- this hour: Blest are they which follow Me. They shall see me face to face and be glad for their knowing. For that shall they enter into this School of learning and prepare themself for the next part of their preparation, which shall be as greater learning wherein they shall know -- and know that they

43

know. This shall bring unto them the privilege of wearing the Crown of Victory -- the Sword of acceptance of Power which shall be given unto them. This shall be given unto them. This shall be given for their preparation and trust which they have earned.

None shall find their way alone. Along the path of truth and justice are the Brothers which are stationed to assist them which have been true unto themself -- that they be assisted in their walk through the dark night of the Soul. Bless these Guardians -- the Brothers which have volunteered to assist thee. Be ye thoughtful of them -- theirs hast been a mission of love and mercy.

To the Recorder:

I am one which hast watched "the way" and picked thee up when ye could not stand, Ye have endured the storms -- the torture of flesh which hast weighed heavily upon thee. Yet thine burden hast been Mine. It is a joyful task that I share with thee, for it is as a day when ye shall walk with Me as one free, and we shall rejoice together and sing the glad anthem which shall ring thruout the Cosmos.

I am one of the Keepers of The Way.

* * * * *

Sori Sori: This is the word I would have thee give unto them this day. There are ones among them which have prepared themself to be brought into this School that I am speaking of. They shall pass among the populace in humility, with the knowledge of who's prepared to be brought in. Too, they shall be as brothers or sisters. The time shall come when the candidate shall come face to face with these brothers which shall bring them to the place of entry. There shall be no display of

44

power -- no haste -- no signs displayed for their approval. It shall be as the acceptance of the heart -- faith in the brother -- that they follow where he leads.

I say unto them which shall be brought in, they shall come unopinionated. Come as a little child -- filled with love and purity. Be ye as one prepared for to enter in - none other shall enter. Give thine whole heart, hand, head unto Me which hast prepared this place for to receive thee. These which enter shall be blest of Me, for I shall receive them as ones prepared. Be ye as ones which tire not, for ye are now being groomed for the entrance which shall be the beginning of the greater part. Be it understood that there are none overlooked, for it is said many times: As ye are prepared so shall ye receive -- it is the law. None escape it.

Be ye as ones which hold high thine banner which I have passed unto thee -- that of the "Cross and Crown". Now some shall say, "What's that? I've never heard of that." Let Me tell thee of Mine banner which I have carried, which hast served Me when I walked as man among men. I was man of flesh and bone. I felt pain, I felt insults, I felt great sorrow and humility. I prayed much for the ones which knew not their inheritance, from whence they came. They were a motley crowd -- the sleepers. I gave of Mineself without recompense.

I walked among them, praying for their deliverance -- speaking that which Mine Father gave unto Me for them. While they professed to understand that which I told them or said, they for the most part gave lip service to Me, that they find favor of Me. Let it be said of the populace this day, they are back. Many remember Me. Many have slept the sleep of illusion, not knowing of their sleep. Many have been dead on their feet -- so deep in sleep that they know not that they are dead. I am now come that they might awaken -- come alive -- knowingly.

Let Me speak of this, "Mine banner". What think ye it is? It is that which ye shall carry within thine heart -- not to display on thy so-called altar for man to gaze upon. It is that which ye have become through thine own effort -- thine own awakening. Ye have traveled the path chosen. Ye have either won or betrayed thineself. It hast been thine, for none hast chosen for thee. When ye have walked the path set before thee in sacrifice -- in honor -- and given of thine love and assistance unto thine fellow man, that he be prepared for his walk in Peace and Light, ye have been as a fellow brother and a hand extended and an example unto him. Ye have taken the insults -- the persecutions gracefully, knowing that there is grace and loving help for each, with no condemnation or judgment. Ye have then worn the symbolic crown of "thorns" -- the cross ye have carried. Thine time is fulfilled. Ye have won thine freedom from the Earth travail. Now ye are the Victor. Ye have won the "Crown of the Victor" -- I say ye have won it! Earned it! None can walk the path thou hast chosen, save thine own self. None shall claim the reward.

* * * * *

Sori Sori; That which goes out shall come in -- it is the rhythm of thine being. That which is sent forth from the center of creation shall return unto its place of origin. It is the law of creation.

* * * * *

When there are sufficient numbers which gather within the Halls of Justice, which are tried and true, I shall show unto them that which I do

46

-- and shall cause to be done. This which I shall show them shall be as nothing done afore time. Now this shall be for the benefit of all mankind. They, the populace, shall know this which I shall bring about through the power which is invested within Me of Mine Father which hast Sent Me. This shall be as part of Mine mission, for it is foreseen that there are ones which shall take up Mine banner and carry it high. These shall be the ones which have answered Mine call. They have awakened -- and when they sit as "One" -- in Council -- one mind - one purpose, I shall make Mineself known unto them.

I shall give unto them instruction -- then there shall be such changes as no man hast seen. There shall be no hunger - no oppression -- each man shall be free. No bondsman shall hold another bondage. There shall be equality among them -- they shall be as brothers, and there shall be love and Light for they shall be enlightened and be as Mine hand and foot made manifest upon the Earth. For this do I come -- for this have I waited.

Be ye as one prepared to do that which I give unto thee to do. Let it be -- let it be as the Father Wills.

* * * * *

That which I give unto thee is for one and all which are seeking the Light, which are the ones which shall hear that which I say and respond unto it. The ones that respond shall be prepared to enter into the place of great learning. Take ye heed, for there is but little time before thine own name is called. Shall ye find that ye have prepared to be brought in? Blest shall they be which find themself acceptable. Be ye not deluded in that which I am saying -- for there is no need to rush and fret, for it is not the way in which to prepare thineself,

I have said many times, Be ye at Peace. "How do I find peace in these troubled times?" I hear them ask. The overcoming of thine own troubles -- therein finding peace. Ye shall look at thine own house. Clean it out, that no darkness lurks within the shadows therein -- no hatred -- no shame to haunt thee -- no hypocrisy -- no self-condemnation -- no criticism of thine Benefactors which keep the way before thee. Ye have been told of these -- know ye of these "Keepers of the Way" which have served thee well in the hours of thine unknowing? Many have given them different names. Yet they are the ones which have volunteered to assist thee silently and lovingly unto the end of thine sojourn. They are greatly blest for their service to mankind. Bear in mind that for them ye might have perished. Be ye not so stupid as to deny that which I say unto thee -- for ye are not so wise that ye can or shall criticize Me. For I Am that I Am -- I Am One with Mine Father, the Source of thine Be-ing.

There are many things which are hidden from thee for thee to find and cherish, which shall bring thee great joy and comfort when ye find them. By thine own preparation shall ye find. It is said: Seek and ye shall find. "Find what?" ye ask. "Thine freedom from bondage," I say -- Is that not worth the effort? Place thine hand in Mine and I shall go all the way with thee. This is Mine word unto thee at this hour -- let it suffice thee.

* * * * *

Sori Sori: When have I forgotten that which I have said? There are none which shall find Me napping.

Let us speak of the work at hand. There are ones which are in a fidget that they know not that which they should do. They have not heard that which I have said unto them. It is given unto some to want me to command their daily lives -- spell it out. Yet I am not prone to such as they expect of Me. I speak in a manner which shall cause them to think for themself. I can not tell them what to think -- nay -- not what to do. I but lead and suggest that they listen unto the small voice within. "How is this done?" they ask, I say unto these which ask: Listen unto that which is within thee -- within thine own breast which beats with rhythm. It is thine sustainer -- that which ye call thine own heart.

There is a time and a place for this revelation wherein it shall be revealed unto thee all that ye shall have need of. Yet ye shall listen -- listen -- listen -- and give thanks that ye have ears to hear. This is thine true communion with thine Source of "Be-ing". Let us give unto thee a parable which shall help in the learning to listen to the Source. Be ye still -- still -- still; place thine hand over thine heart and concentrate upon the rhythm of its beat. Be not weary of the waiting, for it is given unto thee to be as ones which have the impatience of the bee. Ye expect that which ye have not prepared thineself for to receive -- "instant results". Have ye prepared thineself to commune with thine Source? What can thine answer be? When have ye asked of others? Hast thou asked of others? Hast thou asked another for direction?

Be at peace and ask of the cause of thine Being. The Source shall respond unto thine sincere need.

* * * * *

Sori Sori: When the time is come that ye ones which are prepared are brought into this place which is now prepared to receive thee, ye shall be as the ones which have given of thine self for the good of others that they, too, might enter the place of higher learning. For this it is said that

49

none enter unprepared. There shall be the first come. When they are sufficiently prepared, they shall move out into greater fields to greater learning, wherein they shall too serve the younger brothers. For this is the process which serves the purpose of this Plan which is now unfolding before the candidate. For this hast the call gone forth. Prepare for greater revelation which shall be for the good of All. Hast thou heard this call? Hast thou given of thineself that ye be prepared to enter in? Be ye not deluded, for it is a very serious decision to make.

It is given unto Me to see these ones which run to and fro looking for miracles -- giving lip-service to so-called teachers. They prattle phrases of wisdom while they make themself conspicuous by their prattlings, whereby they are none the wiser for they have not yet heard Mine voice. Mine hand they have not touched -- neither have they asked of Me, the Lord God Sent unto mankind for to rescue him from the pit. The pit -- wherein there is only darkness -- no Light -- which is knowledge of thine being -- from whence ye came -- where ye shall go.

These are the things of the greater revelations, which is the part which shall first be shown unto the ones which enter into this School which awaits the candidate. When he is found worthy to enter therein, he shall be greeted with this sign ... which shall be shown unto them. They shall recognize it and they shall hear the word which they have been given aforehand while they have slept.

Be ye alert and give ye thought unto that which I am giving unto thee through this, Mine handmaiden. Be ye not quick to criticize Me -- neither Mine method of communication, for therein is wisdom. I say I know that which I am about. I too know the ones which shall be prepared to enter into this place which awaits them.

Be ye blest to enter, for ye shall find that ye have done thine "homework" sufficiently for thine passport. Let this suffice for this hour.

* * * * *

Sori Sori: This is the new day in which there shall be great and strange new revelations, for many have come into the Earth as Emissaries of the Christ Council. These are among thee this day. They walk as man -- they speak as man -- and they are the manifestation of the Father made flesh. These shall walk softly -- gently -- for the most part unknown among thee. For they are come that the way be made clear for that which shall be done. It is said that "There shall be a great onrush of Light" -- it is so. For this have they come. Be ye not deceived or opinionated about that which is given unto thee through this method. These Emissaries are no myth -- not imagination -- or symbolic. They are the manifestation of the Father made flesh. Can ye hear that which i am saying unto thee this day?

There are things being revealed unto mankind of Earth this day as never before, for this is the day long foretold -- which man has put far in the future, that he be not concerned with that which he shall never have to deal with. "It is not any concern of mine," I hear them say.

Let them sing the song of the foolish and eat unto their fill. Yet I say unto the foolish which think themself wise: Ye have danced thine last mile, for there is no more time for the idiot's delight. The time is at hand when there shall be an accounting, and the sowers shall reap that which they have sown -- for it is an infallible law. For this am I come to gather in Mine flock.

Who is thine flock? some mayhap ask. I say unto these: The ones which have heard Mine call and answered it, for I am the "Good Shepherd". know my "sheep" and they know Mine voice. I lead them back into the fold wherein there is no darkness -- no pain -- no sorrow. Have ye not heard this aforehand? Have ye not traveled far afield since first ye have heard the story? Have ye not slept thru a long night of illusions, and fear consumed thine peace? Have ye not made many turns in the long road which leads back home?

All these things I would have thee ponder, for ye shall be caused to remember them. Ye shall be as one come alive and ask for "Light" which I Am. I shall come as a gentle breeze and touch thee as a peacemaker, which shall comfort and soothe thee. Ye shall see My Light, and no fear shall come unto thee. This I would have thee remember and be not deceived.

For this day I say unto thee, there are many among the populace which make claim; "I am He -- I am He -- God!" These are not of Mine flock, for I say unto thee: The One Sent of the Father boasts not -- neither does he strut himself before man. He moves about quietly -- gently -- for the most part unknown. I reveal Mineself unto them which are ready/prepared for to receive. These shall be as Mine faithful, trusted followers which I call Mine "lambs". Be ye not misled -- for they are not of the "animal kingdom". They shall overcome the animal nature in their preparation for to come into Mine place wherein I abide. Too, it hast been said that the animals shall be changed in this day of enlightenment. The lion and the lamb shall walk together in harmony.

Be ye as one which hast ears to hear Mine words. Ask of Me and I shall respond. While I shall know thine inmost intent, ye shall not make a mockery of thine word -- or Mine word. Thine heart shall be pure, thy hands clean, and thine intent shall be true unto Mine precepts. None deceive Me. Give ye not lip-service to any one which professes to be of the Father sent, which asks of thee pittance for thine salvation. They are not of Me. These have not been sent of Mine Father -- neither have they been called out from among them which walk in darkness.

Be ye as one to discern the true from the false. Let not the one which walks in darkness deter thee from thine walk with Me. For I say unto thee, they do ask of thee thine time -- thine strength and fellowship, in order to enhance their prestige among their fellows of the dark robes. Walk ye with caution -- sure of foot and brave of heart.

Know ye them by their fruit, for they wear two faces -- both are masks. They ask of thee many questions that they might use thee -- that which they can/do use against thee or thine fellows of Light. Some of these are the destroyers. They pilfer their knowledge that they might find their way into the "Secret Place" that they be able to abort the Plan which is of the Light. All these things I would have thee know. Watch for the ones which speak words of deceit -- flattery -- with a velvet tongue. Be not deceived -- neither walk ye in fear. I shall give unto Mine chosen the gift of comprehension. Use it wisely.

* * * * *

Sori Sori: That which hast been written is that which shall be put into a book which shall be given unto the ones which are of the mind to enter into the School of higher learning. These words are designed for them. There are at this time but few which are prepared; therefore, there is no excuse for any delay in getting this portion out to the populace. Small though it be, it shall find its mark. This shall be as a reminder unto them which have begun to stir or awaken.

53

Now this book which is now being closed shall be as the first part of another which shall be added at another time. While this part shall be as a reminder, the next part shall supercede this one -- yet they shall be combined later. It is necessary to prepare them for the next part which shall be of greater proportions -- greater information -- and powerful revelations. First, the awakening for the greater part. It shall be given unto the ones which shall be responsible for its preparation. At the time it is ready for them which are worthy to receive it, it shall be given unto them for the cost of its preparation.

Let this be Mine project at this time. Be ye blest to be Mine hand made manifest. Too, I say blest shall they be which hast given any energy whatsoever unto this Mine project. I forget not Mine servants, for the labor of love is not overlooked. So be it, I lay Mine hand upon thine head and bless thee with Mine being.

Sananda, the Son of God, Sent of Mine Father which hast Sent Me.

* * * * *

Sori Sori: This be Mine word unto them which cry this day: Time is short -- no time for frivolity and wasted energy. Know that while We thine Benefactors are preparing a place for thee that ye might enter into this School of higher learning, that ye might be brought out -- delivered from bondage -- that ye are wasting the precious energy. Precious it is, for it is OUR energy!

Each breath takes thee closer to the end -- the close of thine own cycle -- yea, the collective grand cycle of which ye are part. Consider thine self part of the whole -- responsible for thine part. Art thou not responsible? Hast thou considered thine responsibility? Who shall account for thee, for thine integrity? Are ye so blind as to pass thine responsibility unto thine brother? Wherein hast it been said: Each shall be responsible for every word which proceeds out of his mouth? For he is one within the All. Each is responsible for his own creation for weal or woe.

Hear ye Me in this, for this is no small part of thine awakening or preparation for the next step in thine learning. That which ye have created shall be as thine share -- the harvest ye shall reap. Ponder these words, for they are designed for to awaken thee. Think ye not that they are for thine brother alone. Why thine brother? Art thou not his brother also? Give thought, My beloved children, of thine creation -- 'tis thine to reap even as the great harvest which hast been stored within thine secret place which shall be opened up. What shall ye find therein?

I hear the cries of the little ones yet unborn; I hear the cries of the sick and dying. Hast thou given succor unto these ones? Hast ye given of thine self in loving service that they be comforted -- that they might learn that there is no death -- that there is a place prepared for them? 'Tis a time of soberness, Mine children!

Blest be the one which reaches out a hand that his brother finds his foothold. Yet I say unto one and all, be ye appraised of thine sowing, for there is a time of reaping. While I see them which think themself wise going to and fro with that which they think to be their passport into "heaven" crying, "Follow me! Come, follow me -- I am the way -- I have him! I know! I have seen him. Come, I can lead thee unto him."

O, ye which have no enlightenment, I come as one which is sent of Mine Father that ye be enlightened of Him. It is said: Pray ye for comprehension, that ye know the true from the false. I call thine attention unto these things that ye be not deceived by their honeyed words -- their loud, boisterous claims. Know them, My beloved ones, with thine heart.

Ye have been apprised how to find thine contact with Me -- thine Source of Being! Ye have been told to listen -- listen with thine whole heart. Hast thou heard Me -- that which I have said? Why put Me aside as one speaking unto thine friend -- thine neighbor -- not unto thee? Yet ye run hither and yon to touch the false prophet. Give ye thought of thine Source, My children, for all thine sorrows come from thine forgetting "It" -- thine Source. Now the time is come to awaken. Come forth as one prepared to walk in the Light which I Am. Therein is enlightenment -- therein is eternal freedom!

For this have I come this day that ye sleepers might awaken. Hast thou stirred? What voice hast thou followed, Mine children? I ask of thee, what voice hast thou followed? Where hast thou found freedom? Where hast thou found Peace? Let thine cares be for all thine brothers which struggle along the path which ye walk, while thine own eye be blinded. Reach out unto thy Benefactors, which are also reaching out a helping hand that ye find thy way. Art thou doing as much for thine brother which knows not his Benefactors? Be ye his, even as They are unto thee. Remember, as ye give so shall ye receive. What shall that be? Give unto Me thine hand and ye shall not be misled, for I am the Light of thine life -- the Light that never fails.

* * * * *

Sori Sori: This day there shall be a gathering-in which shall be as none other -- ever! There are ones which have awakened unto the Light which is the power -- the strength of the ages. It is new unto man of

56

Earth. He has two choices: Either he arises and chooses the Light -- or remains in darkness to repeat his sorry way again, until he hast made the choice to come into the Light of his own free will.

We, the Host, hast prepared the place -- furnished the energy -- offered unto him the cup of freedom. It is his choice to make this day. This is the day of decision, for long have We waited this day for man to stir from his slumber.

* * * * *

Sori Sori: While there are ones which deny Me Mine authority, even Mine handmaidens, I say unto one and all, it bothers Me not, for they are as the unknowing ones -- yea, the sleepers. These are the walking dead -- yet they shall cry out for assistance 'ere it is finished. They shall find their false gods will not comfort them in the time of sorrow. Let them sleep on. Fret not thine self, for they are as a foul wind which blows its way out -- passes as a foul breeze. They shall have their day of awakening. Be ye at peace.

* * * * *

Sori Sori: There is but one Light -- the Light Eternal. This is the Power of "our parent" which is the Source of Being in which all exists. No thing exists without, for there is no without -- no place other than within It/Him which we might call the "Father" -- the "All" -- the "S". He is and ever shall be the Eternal parent, or Source of Being, the Eternal Light of all existence. For that ye shall awaken unto thine Source -- Our Source wherein ye have slept the sleep of forgetfulness. This is the end of thine illusions. The day hast now come when ye shall come to know as I know -- as We of the Host know. Yet we come unto thee in love and great compassion that ye come into the fullness of thine inheritance, which is the knowing of thine inheritance. To know is Wisdom. Ye have long dwelt in the shadow -- the thinker's realm of illusion -- confusion -- suffering and sorrow.

Now We call thee home. We seek thee out and guide thee -- assure thee that there is a Light -- that which ye are part. A cell within the One which is not divided into parts -- even as thine own physical body is one -- while it is made up of many cells which ye are not aware of. Yet without one member thy body would not be whole -- yes? no? Think ye on these things, I say unto thee -- one and all. Yet ye cannot comprehend the <u>All</u> -- the Cosmos -- the Eternal things which are within this, which we see as All One. Therefore, because I Am, thou art also. This I would have thee ponder.

Let thine mind dwell upon these things I speak unto thee -- yea, they are but words designed for thine thinking mind. It is written, "Let the mind which is in Me, be the mind which is in thee." It is now come when We of the Host have come nigh unto thee that ye comprehend these things of which We speak, which is but a fragment or the beginning of thine learning. For thou couldst not endure the greatest of truth -- the Light of all truth. For this hast it been revealed in parts and symbols -- that ye might become prepared for greater revelation, which is our purpose at this time. This is Mine purpose of this little book now being presented unto thee at the behest of the Mighty Council. For it is given in the purest of love and intention -- that of bringing thee out of bondage -- making known unto thee thine true heritage. So be ye as one prepared to receive that which we have for thee. Ye shall be truly blest to receive of Our love and assistance.

* * * * *

58

Sori Sori: It is with Mine own hand that this portion hast been given unto thee for them which shall find it. Some shall find it for the effort they have put forth; some shall have it placed within their hand; some shall throw it aside in denial. Yet I say unto thee, Mine handmaiden, thou hast done thine part -- now they shall do theirs. Let not thine heart be troubled for them which deny that which is given, for it is not thine part to nurse them as infants. For when the mother bird places the food in the wee one's mouth, they ingest it. So let it be well with the ones which have ears to hear -- eyes to see. Let it be well with thee, for there is the reward for work well done. Sori Sori: Ye shall now bring to a close this part of thine assignment, for there is greater work to be done. So be it and Selah.

* * * * *

Sori Sori: Come to Me unopinionated with empty hands. Clutch nothing unto thine self -- for ye own nothing. Boast not of thine possessions. There is nothing which binds thee unto the world of matter save thine opinions -- preconceived ideas which have been handed down for many millennia. Now I say unto one and all these past opinions and preconceived ideas have become legirons -- which hold thee bound. I say ye are bound by thine thinking. Many think themself wise when they are learned of man. This is but his opinion preconceived by others' opinions, wherein others elaborate upon the other man's opinions.

Wherein hast he been learned of his Source? Wherein hast he found his freedom? Wherein hast he been enlightened? This I would ask of thee, O man of Earth: Have ye found freedom from oppression, pain, sorrow, hunger? Wherein hast thou cast thine seed? Wherein hast thou reaped? Can ye answer Me, or hast thou forgotten in thine wayward and riotous way, wherein ye have fallen from grace? Know ye that ye live and breathe by Mine Father's grace? Hast thou given thought unto thy Source of Being? What of thine own understanding of thine Source? Do ye know to whom ye pay allegiance? To whom dost thou turn in the time of sorrow? To whom dost thou owe allegiance? Think ye are wise?

I ask thee how many times hast thou walked the Earth in flesh? What remember thou of these walks? What hast thou remembered -- learned from or through them? I say unto thee, for the most part thou hast walked blindly -- stumbling -- falling. While ye have cried out for help, to whom, to what hast thou cried out -- remember? Wherein comes thine cry? Hast thou remembered when thou hast been picked up, fed, comforted, healed, and set upon thine path which ye have chosen? Remember, my child, thou art not so wise!

While I am saying unto thee -- awaken and come alive, what art thou saying to Me? What is thine opinion unto Me? I need no man's opinion, for I know him even as he is -- not by the color of skin or dress -- I know him by his Light. Let me say again, no man knows himself as I know him.

It is now come that he shall awaken unto his Source and be as one come alive -- for he hast slept overtime. For this have We of the Host of Light entered into the affairs of man -- man of Earth, for his abiding place -- Earth -- is in a precarious position. We are calling thy attention unto this for the purpose of alerting thee unto thine actions and preparation for that which shall come upon thee. Ye have been filled with all sorts of ideas and false concepts -- denials of thine origin and inheritance willed unto thee of the "Source". Ye have looked in dark places for comfort -- relief from thy many woes which ye have brought about -- upon thyself.

Now it is come when We of the Host hast made ourself known. Do ye receive us -- of us -- of our "expertise" -- our wisdom and love -- or art thou still asleep? Listen, listen, o man of Earth! I say unto thee the day of accounting is upon thee! Alert thyself and come unto the Light, wherein is comfort, peace and safety. Fear not, for I am not a traitor. I am one of the Angelic Host which art thine Benefactors. For us, We of the Host, thou hast been spared for this day. Be ye as one willing to follow the Light which we are. Seek the Light. Ask thine Source for comprehension and accept it as a gift of the Father. So shall ye be lifted up, and then ye shall sing His praise and be filled with joy.

So be it -- I have spoken in His Name. I AM that which I AM.

* * * * *

Sori Sori: This day let us speak of the ones which have been tried and found true -- those which have given of themself in the Light of loving service unto their fellow man. I ask of them, are ye as one prepared to follow where I lead thee? Or art thou contented to remain wherein ye are? Art thou satisfied with that which ye are about -- that which ye think is the best ye are capable of doing? Wouldst thou commit thine time and energy to other patterns of life -- which would entail a separation from family, friends, familiar settings? Wouldst thou follow Me without question? I await thine answer truly.

* * * * *

Sori Sori: Say I unto them which have ears to hear, that I have brought forth this little book that they might come to know that I am not a figment of someone's imagination -- that I am in the place wherein I am fully prepared to give unto them as they are prepared to receive. When they are prepared, I shall reach out and touch them as a fellow brother -- with hand of flesh and blood -- for I am the one which is free from all limitation. I can take any form I will for Mine purpose.

Now, Mine purpose is to make known unto the children of Earth that which they have not known -- that they might awaken unto the power and glory of that which is theirs. This is Mine purpose, and the Father's Will. I am sent that the child of Earth be prepared to return with Me unto his true estate. So let it be. I have given of Mine self, Mine love and energy that it be so. So let it be for thine own good that ye hear and respond unto it in love and wisdom.

Recorded by Sister Thedra

PART II

Sori Sori -- Beginning this day we shall give unto thee this portion, which shall be put with that which was finished yesterday as an addition to it, shall I say, as it shall be two parts, yet one cover.

It shall have or carry this name: "Mine Intercom Messages from the Realms of Light" -- which shall carry the name I gave unto thee -- Sister Thedra.

So let us go on with it.

* * * * *

Sori Sori: By Mine own hand shall I pen these documents, which shall be added unto that book finished on the yesterday. Truly it is a new day -- the day of the great awakening when many shall come to know me as I am. These which come to know Me shall be as ones lifted up. They shall dwell with me as One with Me. They shall be as the ones which have the will to go with Me wherein I go. These shall come from the four corners of the Earth, for Mine hand I have stretched out into the far reaches of the Cosmos that they be awakened.

For the time is come when the Earth shall give unto them no footing, no comfort. So let it be understood that I am the Lord God which does speak unto all people, that they be blest to come into Mine place of abode -- that they be spared that which shall come upon the Blessed Mother Earth as she gives birth to the moon which she shall bear as a Second Son. Be ye as ones which hear that which I am saying unto thee at this hour, for there is no time -- for today is the "now". Now is the day of decision -- for this am I calling from the heights,

63

Hear Me and give unto Me thine hand and heart, and ye shall rejoice that ye have responded unto Mine call. So be it and Selah.

Since there is but little time, I shall put these words with the other just finished. They carry with them blessings from the realms of Light in which ye live and have thine being. Behold ye the hand of God, the Father, move, for He it is which hast given unto thee Being -- Life -- Life of His Life. The breath which ye breathe is His breath. The ebb and flow is His breath -- even as the tides of thine ocean -- incoming -- outgoing flow -- which is the rhythm of creation.

There are no things which are exempt from this law of energy inflow and outflow. Yet it is constant chance which is beyond thy present comprehension. It is upon this in and outflow which carries the manifestation of Earth, in and out of physicality. The rest is the outflow, (rest is what ye call death) when one lays aside his physical form. The inflow is when he takes physical form of flesh.

His rest within the higher realms of Light is his time of learning and preparing himself for his next place of learning. For it is a general ongoing process -- this Life of Life -- the progression is an ongoing process. Now that ye are within the New Dispensation, it is necessary that each and every man or manifestation be as one prepared for thy new part -- which shall be new and strange unto the one unprepared. It is for this that I have made Mine self known unto man of Earth. I am speaking in the language which man can and shall understand -- each shall understand in his own tongue.

Let this be unto thee great understanding, for it is now expedient that each and all shall come to understand the cause of their sojourn upon this beautiful planet ye call "Earth". Now let Me assure thee that this planet shall not be destroyed. For this hast there come from out the distant corners of the firmaments great and powerful ones prepared to assist in her birthing process. As she gives birth unto her son, so does she be birthed -- raised into another octave of existence, which ye know not.

By Mine own hand shall I give unto her a new berth which is now prepared for her. Was it not written that "There shall be a new Heaven and a new Earth"? It is now upon thee. Be ye not afraid, for there are provisions made for each and every one which hears and answers Mine call. So be ye as one wise -- to be as one wise -- and come follow where I lead thee. For this am I calling unto them which have a will to come -- blest shall they be.

Let Me speak unto them which call themself "Christian". Be ye not swift or careless in denying Me, for I am the Living "Christus -- Christo", Sent of the Source of All Life. This, Our Source, is that from which All Life -- Light -- IS. Nothing which exists is without "It" -- "Him". He is not divided -- He/It is inclusive of the "All". Ye may rightly call "it" Father, even as I -- yet I know Him to be that which is the "All". Yet who among thee understands that which I am saying? For so long have ye limited thineself unto Mine sayings of yesteryear, even though many of these have undergone many changes -- some unrecognizable.

Now I say unto thee, one and all, I bring unto thee this day a new commandment. Awaken ye from thine deep sleep and follow where I lead thee. Lay down thine precept and opinions of Me. Know ye that I am Come to bring unto thee freedom from bondage. Be ye up and about the Father's business! Give up thine way of the drunkard; walk ye sober and know ye which way to go, for I shall direct thee. Lay down thine burdens and I shall free thee from them. Let thine heart be softened -- thine hand to help thine brothers. Give unto the starving food and drink. Bind up the wounds which have the pain and suffering.

Give solace unto the dying, which know not from where they came -- neither whither they go. <u>Tell them..."There is no death</u>," for this is the message that I gave unto them on the mount. Did they hear it? Have they not preached "<u>Hell -- Damnation</u>" -- held them in bondage and fear? Wherein have they taught that there is forgiveness -- a glorious heritage awaiting them -- the <u>rhythm</u> of <u>life</u> -- No Death! Just One with the All -- preparation for the next step - not the end.

There is no end, for each and every "entity" goes at his own pace as he is prepared. From glory unto glory -- by his own will. None brings him -- it is against the Law.

Let it be understood that there is no place wherein the Light cannot go. Yet the ones which are within the pits of darkness call out and the ones of Light find them. And as they are prepared and willing they are delivered up -- put into the proper place, wherein they are with their own kind -- be it thief -- murderer -- or saint. For this is the law: As ye prepare thyself, so do ye receive. Even so, there is justice for all. So be it by the Grace of the Father-Mother and Son which I Am.

Let us speak unto them which hast not the mind to give unto Me credit for being that which I Am. These shall come to know -- these shall cry for Mine mercy and grace. Yet, I say unto them, <u>first forgive thyself of all thy transgressions</u>, and make haste to correct them. Then one shall be sent to assist thee in thine climb or ascent. Be ye not concerned which one I shall send -- for ye know them not. Yet ye shall be as one joyful to receive these ones which are so merciful -- which give of themself that others might be brought out.

Have ye been taught of the way of heavenly messengers which are the "Watchers of The Way", which stand ready to assist thee when you call with a pure intent? They are thy Benefactors. Do ye give unto them credit for that which they are? They are ever watchful for thee and await thy recognition. Yet, there are ones which deny them and when they are in pain they cry out unto their unknown god.

From whence comest thou, Mine little ones? From whence cometh thou? Wherein hast thou found peace? Wherein hast thou been comforted? Why wait until ye think ye are going into the unknown in despair -- fearful and without the knowledge or the Light which sustains thee? These are the things I would have thee ponder -- in thine haste, or meditations.

Let it be understood that I am the one which walked the way of the initiate in the land of the Jew in ages past. I walked as man among men. Yet Mine words were not heeded, for the greater part of the populace cared not for Mine teaching, the word I brought. They resisted Me -- denied Me -- Mine part -- yet I forgave their unknowing -- their transgressions. For I knew Mine Source of Being -- from whence I came. I knew that Mine Father and I were One -- even as ye are One with Him. This I would have thee know, and ponder long upon that which I shall give unto thee -- for I have not given of Mine storehouse yet. I am not weary of Mine place of assignment.

Mine time is now at hand. It is said I did not finish Mine Earth mission in the time past -- yet never have I left thee. It is Mine time with thee now that ye be brought into the fullness of thine inheritance.

So be it as the Father Wills. I come as the deliverer -- the wayshower. Yet I bring with Me a great Host which have given of their energy, even as I have, that thy Mother Earth be brought into her new berth within the firmament. So be it; it shall be done. It shall be done as the Father Wills! He hast willed it -- I have said it! So shall it be.

Now, Mine children which heard that which I have said, shall find that I remember that which I have said -- and I am true unto Mine word. I keep Mine covenant with them which have given theirs unto Me. We are as one in that "covenant", for we are of one mind, one intent -- that of finishing our mission and returning unto our Source. Be it so -- so let it be as the Father Wills.

It hast been recorded that there shall be a great homecoming -- a great festival. We of the Host have prepared the table where ye shall be brought. It shall be filled with guests from a far distance which lend their wisdom, joy and love. There shall be such joy as man has never known. Let this be Mine time with thee -- Mine expression of love and mercy which shall be as Mine word manifest.

For I say unto thee, not one thing which man hast done, made or invented could convey unto thee such an array of Beings and their parts which shall be added unto Mine -- such as hast never before been. Now it is come when there shall be a new heaven and a new earth, for it is foretold -- the time of fulfillment is now come,

Many shall go through the "death experience". It is for the purpose of learning that there is <u>no death</u>. How else could they truly know? Did I not say it? Now let this be known among the populace that I am come that they know Me this day as one of them. I have walked the way set before them. Have I not known sorrow and suffering?

Now I come with a glad shout, "Look up -- thine salvation is at hand!" See that which goes on about thee. Ask to see and know -- for there is no need to ask to see if ye hold thine hands before thine eyes. I say, Look to See -- be ye not fearful, for greater things shall there be for to see -- and to learn.

* * * * *

Sori Sori: This is the time spoken of in thine holy scripts -- when they shall be plagued with all sorts of plagues -- when the dark ones shall come from out the pit -- when there shall be great sorrow and torment. The streets shall be red with blood -- hast it not been written? I have come at this time that ye be as one spared such sorrow. Art thou prepared to go with Me all the way? I ask of thee again, art thou prepared to go all the way with Me? I wait thine answer.

Consider well what thine answer shall be before ye say, "Yea Lord!" For to commit thine self and default thine commitment is to betray thine own self. He is the worst of traitors, for it is no small deed of unknowing -- it is "sin" as ye would understand. Ye have used that word without understanding. When one professes to know that which I say unto him, and in his haste to please Me or to make known <u>himself</u> unto the populace, he ofttimes in his haste -- and ego -- Speaks without knowing that which I shall ask of him.

He gives no thought of that which he shall be asked to do. Then when he finds that there is sacrifice entailed -- he finds it too exacting. I hear him say: "O, but I couldn't do that! I cannot be both father, mother and son -- I can't do that, for I have no training for that; I am not wise in the way of the initiate; I have no degree -- I am not enlightened in the way of things of spirit. I do not belong to this or that group or organization."

Now I see them as children -- untrained, undisciplined -- asking for a position which they are not prepared for to fill. This is that for which this School which I have spoken of hast been established, hast been set up, that the ones which have the true abiding desire to follow in the way I point shall be prepared to go the whole way with Me. For it is necessary that they -- or thee -- be as one prepared to follow in the way I go. Now I say unto one and alt: Ye shall be fully prepared for to enter in -- into the place wherein I abide. None other shall -- can enter -- it is the law. I ask, art thou ready to come with Me into this School of training, whereby ye might be prepared to be brought out of darkness -- bondage -- where ye might be forever free?

Now this day is a time of decision, for it is so written that time is come when "Mother" Earth shall give unto thee no comfort, no footing. For this have I made a place wherein ye might be prepared for greater learning -- greater service, unto thine calling. This is our part, our purpose, our choice, that we come at this propitious time that ye be offered that choice -- either to follow the Light or remain in bondage.

I hear some voice from out the darkness cry out for his freedom. Yet another asks, "What is this I hear? This bondage stuff? I'm free. I can do that which I choose. See that which I possess? Am I not rich? I own all I desire -- I am great among men -- I am healthy -- why should I fear anything?" I say unto this one, be ye not puffed up. Be ye not so foolish as to think ye are exempt from the law of thine being.

It is said: "The Earth is Mine, and the fullness thereof." Ye are guest in Mine house. The Earth hast been a gift which ye have been privileged to share for a season. What say ye of thine time spent upon this planet ye call "Earth". Hast thou given thought unto thine status -- unto her, thine hostess -- Benefactor? Or have ye been one of the laggards -- slothful and caring not for thine part or obligation unto that which hast been thine dwelling place for a season?

This I would have thee, one and all, consider well before ye make answer unto Me -- for ye deceive Me not. I am not deceived by any one or thing. I am the one which hast gone the long way to provide a place of safety for thee. "What is there to lose?" ye ask. I say unto thee, thine Eternal Freedom.

O, ye of darkness -- ye slothful ones which have danced -- eaten of the flesh of the carcass -- sung the songs of the lowest vibration which gives thee great mysterious passion which is beyond thy control -- ye have called it "fun" -- even happiness.

Yet I declare unto thee this day the "vibes" are destructive unto thine inner body. Thine hand hast begun to shake -- thine voice to quiver -- thine ears decline to register the sweet tones of the wind. Ye hear not the song of the lark -- for thou hast not known that which ye do.

For ye have contrived ways and means of working up the passions of the lower body which hast been thy only part of self ye have known. While ye have been dancing -- eating -- drinking -- ye have not paid heed unto that which ye shall do on the morrow. It is given unto many to find they are in a new, strange environment wherein they are lost - crying out for direction -- no Light to guide them. Yet they are not free to do that which they did yesterday, for they have lost their physical

71

body -- how? How? ye ask. Do ye, these ones, not remember? Where wast thou last? O yes, <u>now</u> I <u>remember</u> -- what remorse!!

O, Mine precious, listen, and heed, for it is a time of awakening. I say unto thee, ye are precious in Mine sight. I have provided for thee -- I have a plan for thee. Now I call thee -- Come, and I shall show unto thee that which shall bring thee joy which shall be lasting, and ye shall suffer no more the remorse of the wayward. Can ye hear Me? Have ye asked to hear Me? Ask, and I shall come unto thee in love and Light for to bring thee into the Light of great understanding of thine eternal being.

* * * * *

Sori Sori: This be a time of devotion and soberness. For as I speak these words, I see from Mine vantage point the ones which are looking for substance within the alleyways and back doors. Have ye seen this pitiful sight? Have ye given thought unto them? I remind thee: The time comes when there shall be naught for the dogs -- neither for the master -- no morsel for <u>his</u> belly. Fear not, for I say unto thee there shall be provision in Mine place of abode for them which prepare themself for to enter. Hast thou heard that which I have said? If not, it would behoove thee to give thought to that which I have caused to be recorded thru this, Mine hand-maiden.

Be ye not so foolish as to deny Me -- neither Mine word -- for I come fully prepared to give unto thee, one and all, as they are prepared to receive. Wherein have ye given unto Me credit for being that which I am? That which I have said is for all' which have a mind to go all the way with Me. Some ask, "How far is the way I must go?" O foolish ones of little knowledge -- ye think thyself wise! Yet ye know not that ye stand on the brink of destruction. I am come as a loving Father-Brother-Friend, bringing a Host of Enlightened Ones with Me that thy foothold upon the Earth and her inhabitants be spared. For in truth, there swiftly comes the hour when this blessed planet shall reel and rock -- then she shall throw off the laggards, even as the dog shakes water from his back.

Let us speak frankly and truly ye and I. I ask of thee, think ye I am that which I am? Or do ye think I am an entertainer, playing some prank for thine amusement? Answer ye Me. Know ye that ye have not dreamed of that which is in our place of abode -- such apparatus as man of Earth has never conceived of. Our monitor system is as one which can scan any place within existence and hear thine every word -- see thine thought. Our system leaves nothing to imagination or wished for. Yet there are ones playing games -- thinking to deceive Me -- Us.

Poor unlearned ones, for we do attempt to reach them even as they slumber upon thine cold streets. We have pity for them -- as the unknowing helpless of thy social system. Yet I say unto all which concern themself, be ye as ones thoughtful of these ones, for perhaps ye might be one of them. Be ye not so puffed up! Hast it not been recorded herein that ye are but a guest upon this little orb? Ye own nothing! Ye are but a pilgrim in a strange land.

Give ye thought of these things, for it is the better part of wisdom. I come not as a prophet of doom - I have heard it said! Yet there is a difference, is there not? The ones which come as the dark brothers give unto thee no hope -- no alternative. I bring unto thee a Plan, simple as it is, asking naught of thee save obedience unto the Cosmic Law -- which is plainly and simply placed within thine hand. Ye cannot say,

"I have not seen, or heard it", for it is our intent that ye do hear, and know. For it is thine own decision which ye will choose.

I offer Mine hand unto the blind, the sick, the lame, and say, Arise - Come! I shall be unto thee thine comforter. Yet, he shall hold Mine hand and WILL to arise. Good Shepherd am I. While I simply watch in loving patience with justice for all, I simply give unto thee of Mine love and energy, that ye be prepared for the day of sorrow -- or joy. Which way, Mine child? Which way shall ye choose? Here is Mine hand in love. Fear not -- be at peace and follow Me. For I am One with the Father Mother God. I am the Son Sent that ye might return unto thine rightful place wherein ye shall find eternal peace.

* * * * *

Sori Sori: This hour I see the ones which are mimicking Me. These are the ones which think themself wise -- these are the ones which betray themself -- these are the ones which cause confusion and betrayal. It is said the ones which polly-parrot the words of the uninitiated -- the unknowing ones -- are deceived; unto these I would speak at this hour. There are none so sad as the one which thinks himself wise.

When one sets himself up and asks of thee, "Follow me -- I am the one which hast the cure -- the power to save" -- and asks of thee alms - gives unto thee potions, or talisman, for thine release from thy woes, give him naught. Give unto him naught, for he is but an impostor. Ne'er does the initiated ask of thee aught save adherence unto the law of love.

Bring thine self to the "altar" of the Living God, and know ye it is within thee -- within thine own breath. 'Tis not built of stone and mortar! It is within thine own heart cell. Be ye not deluded by the ones which are prone to hold thee in bondage, it is the way of the unenlightened. Ask of the Light -- the Source of thine being, and then listen unto that which is the beat, the rhythm of the heart. I say unto thee, ye shall hear, for ye shall ask with sincerity of purpose and for the good of all mankind, for none other can hear the wee small voice within. This is thy Oneness with the All -- the Light of the World -- the I AM Presence -- which is ever present. To know is wisdom.

So be it, I shall speak unto thee and ye shall hear Me when ye are prepared to receive Me. Yet ye are prone to demand that which ye have imaged Me to be. I say unto one and all, ye have been "hoodwinked". Ye have been given false impressions of Me -- of thine Source of being -- yea, even of thine own self. I am sent of Mine Father Eternal that ye might come to have knowledge of thine self -- thine oneness with Him -- it -- the Everness -- of Life Eternal. So be it and Selah.

* * * * *

Sori Sori: There be ones which know not that I Am. There be ones which walk with Me, and others which are Mine peers -- those which are even as I am which are Mine brothers. These are the "Elders", the ones which have gone before thee that ye be given life. For long hast they, the Elders, been the pointers of The Way. Know ye what I am saying unto thee? Nay, ye do not, for ye hast not been enlightened on this which I shall give unto thee.

I shall tell thee a portion which is new unto thee. Ye shall come to know that which I say to be of great value unto thee, for ye shall be as ones to learn of thine lineage. This is part of that which ye shall learn within the School of which I have spoken. Therein ye shall be appraised of such as shall give unto thee great power -- and joy. For to know is of the utmost importance. And it is power rightly used. Speaking of power, when thy understanding is reached, the Light is all-consuming. This is power -- power to create in the Father's likeness.

This is as that which is beyond thine present comprehension. Yet it is that which ye shall come to comprehend as truth in its fullness, its totality. Thou hast perhaps wondered about these things of which I shall speak. Yet it is beyond thine ken of understanding at this moment. Let us explore these subjects further, wherein ye shall learn that ye have not yet touched the "hem of thine Father's garment", so vast it is!

Shall ye be prepared to go all the way with Me on this exploration? Shall ye be as Mine guest? I am giving thee Mine invitation. I extend unto thee Mine hand. I give unto thee of Mine love and energy. Ye shall have the Will. This is thine passport. There are no laggards on this journey into the unknown. Come with Me, and ye shall be glad. Mine children hast not glimpsed such joy and wonderment as they which walk with Me on the exploration. Can ye image the way in which i go, without the baggage which encumbers thee?

Hast it not been given unto thee to look at the Milky Way of the heavens and ask, "What is up there?"

Mine child, ye shall be shown when ye walk with Me. Have ye not heard Mine words? I have said unto thee I am not limited. I know no limitation. The Milky Way is as a carpet for Mine feet. Yet I walk not upon it. I know it as ye know thine dwelling place.

The wonderment of it would be too great for the uninitiated. This is the portion which shall be given unto the ones which are prepared for to go all the way with Me, for we shall chart well our course and ye shall be able to comprehend that which ye see and hear. Ye shall feel such joy as ye hast not known. So be it and Selah.

Come unto me and be ye free from the attraction of the moon and the gravitation of the Earth. Then we shall rejoice at the wonderment of it all -- the work of the Father's hand. <u>Then</u> ye shall sing, "How Great Thou Art." Give unto Me credit for knowing that which I am, that which I am about -- <u>that is to bring thee out of bondage</u>. Then ye shall know that which I mean when I say unto thee, I come that ye be free from all thine blindness -- thine bondage -- unknowing -- thine loneliness. Hast thee not longed to fly unto the stars -- explore the Milky Way? Hast thou imaged it! O, the grandeur of it! O blessed Father, let it be! Let it be me. Have ye taken thought of the wonder of it all?

Let us ponder it and rejoice, for it shall be a joyous journey, Mine child! Let it be for this am I speaking. Be ye as one with me and I shall be thine Host. Abide with Me -- happy journey!!

* * * * *

When ye have been within this place wherein I am, ye shall be as one to praise the Source of thine being for the glory and beauty. Ye shall know that ye are one with it. There shall be a glad welcome, for ye shall know us here as we know thee. Long have we awaited thine coming. So be it that there are many heavenly bodies to see and things to learn -- for there are the galaxies which ye see not from our point of view. Until we meet, beloved, be at peace.

I am one of the crew of the Starship.

* * * * *

77

Sori Sori: When ye have been brought into the Starship, ye shall have all thy needs supplied. There shall be such provision as is suitable unto the occasion, and ye shall be free to partake or reject -- for it shall be as a "beautiful party" which shall be as none thou hast seen.

Give ye thanks this day is come. Let us join in the glad refrain -- Hallelujah! Hallelujah! For it is come This Day!

Blest art they which are prepared to sing this praise unto the Source of our being.

* * * * *

Sori Sori: Bless thine self and let all be blest which ask of thee to hear the story which is unfolding before thee. <u>Call not</u> unto them to listen. Yet when they come, they shall be given it as I am giving it unto thee, for it shall be told thruout the land. Yet ye shall <u>not</u> call them out of their beds to "deliver a speech". They shall find it, and be ye as one to give it forth even as one of yesterday that wast given them. Even they rebelled and cried against thee. They shall come to know that they are the fools, crying in the darkness. They shall be as the traitors. And the dark-robed ones shall call thee names, which shall not touch thee, for I shall set Mine hand against them. Be ye blest this day.

For they, the dark-robed ones, shall find thee and torment thee for their own purpose -- the penny. Be ye as one quiet and silent, and feign not wisdom; for they, the dark brothers, shall lay in wait for thee. Give unto them naught that they can misuse -- use against thee, I speak from the higher realms. I see them as vultures seeking out the carrion. Be ye no part of them. Now it is come when ye shall come to understand that

78

which I have shown unto thee concerning these ones which we refer to as the dark-robed ones.

Care not for thine self. Fear naught, for I am with thee unto the end. Blest are they which walk with Me.

* * * * *

Sori Sori: The coming in and going out is necessary at this time, for the end of the age is upon thee. While ye but notice the signs and outer manifestations, we at this point see the greater conditions which shall be brought about. For it is indeed a birthing process.

Do ye understand that which is meant by "birthing process"? There shall be born from the womb of the Earth Mother a Son -- which shall rip, tear, and be painful unto her body. There shall be an embryo -- tender and fragile, follow the birth. Ye shall know this as an "after-birth", and it shall fall back upon the place from whence the Earth hast rested in the firmament. This shall be as a small, unmatured, imperfect, undeveloped moon. Now this shall fall from the womb after the "babe," or new moon leaves the womb. As she is yet in the throes of the birth pains, this shall cause/ or result in the lurching, tossing, convulsing of Mother Earth. For this art there many attendants -- many "scientists" which have come from out the Cosmos to give of themself in the effort to lessen the pain. Need I try to explain the unexplainable unto ye children which are not yet awake?

I say unto thee, for this great Cosmic event, we of the Light realms are awaiting with great anticipation and care -- for it is fortuned us to be the ones which see that which shall follow this Cosmic event. Could ye but see, ye would be up and about thine own part of this "great event", even though ye could not know the fullness thereof. By Mine own hand I have devised a Plan for the children of the planet upon which ye now have footing, and too, the Plan includes the living creatures which I have caused to be born or given life at this season.

Be ye not concerned for them which ye love -- for I love them more. I have prepared for them too. It is no concern of thine, for Mine is the perfect Plan -- it shall not fail. By the power which is invested within Me of the Source of Being shall this plan be brought into its fullness, which shall be that which hast been spoken of as the "Golden Age".

Can ye envision this? Nay, ye are not prepared for such as shall be brought about in this birthing process! There is no word -- no possibility that I could cause one of ye inhabitants upon the planet to fully comprehend such as this birthing shall bring about. This is known unto us as the Light-bearing mother, which is bringing forth her child unto the altar of the Living God for its baptism and blessing.

Know ye that which is meant by the baptism? -- which is known as the Christening, I believe? Know ye the meaning of the Christening?

Bless thine self, and I shall tell thee that which ye can comprehend. For the time approaches quickly when ye shall remember the story I shall give unto thee in "mini" form, that ye might have a small glimmer of the great Wonder of it all. So be it and Selah.

* * * * *

Sori Sori: It is foreseen that there shall be great glaciers melt and the water shall be misplaced. And for this there shall be a great change in the weather and the patterns and balancing of the Earth -- which shall cause great displacement of the people which are in the lands to the north. Too, it shall affect the economy of the world. Therefore, we say unto all which have an interest in such things, be ye alert. Put not thy physical body in danger, for ye are needed at this time for the balancing of Mother Earth. Know ye that ye do help? Know ye this? And why?

For there are ones which have come for to lend their energy at this time which is come. Each hast been put, or ye might say "planted" in certain places -- for a purpose which ye know not. When ye, or they, go to and fro at random of thine own will, ofttimes it causes a disturbance in the patterns. Therefore, there might be a suffering of the physical form. This we would not will for thee.

Be ye as ones which shall ask for wisdom, and it is wisdom to have direction from the ones which <u>know</u>. We see clearly, for we are well equipt. For we have been long at observing the Earth and her moon. It is now come when there shall be a new moon within the firmament, and it shall be as one with the Mother Earth -- as the mother ewe and her lamb. She shall nurse her offspring and bring it to maturity, and then it shall, too, be populated as a new generation.

A new people shall be planted upon it, even as the present "hu-man" was upon the "Mother Earth". For this shall be the fortune of the ones which have betrayed themself. Then they shall begin anew from the beginning. No science shall they have -- no knowledge of their former existence within the places of Earth wherein they went their willful way in self-betrayal and denial of their true heritage. This shall be justice, as there is justice for all. So be it, as they are prepared so shall they receive.

Each shall take with them that which hast tormented them, and be as their judge -- their own tormentor. These shall begin at the beginning. They shall have no memory of the past -- their sciences, their art, music, "culture" -- not even their children or kin. Their memory shall be blanked from them from the beginning.

Yet they, too, shall in season weary of their lot and cry out for Light and strength. They shall earn their bread by the sweat of their brow and work the soil upon their knees with their bare hands.

While We of the Host shall await their time of maturity, we shall be prepared to give unto them of our love and strength, even as we have done with ye which have prepared thine self for to be brought out. This shall be Mine intention to fetch them as soon as they cry out, "Father, have mercy!"

* * * * *

Sori Sori: With these words ye shall be blest; for that I am speaking. I speak unto one and all, that there be Light within them.

For this are We of the Mighty Council giving of our strength and love. We art asking of them naught other than they listen and heed that which we say, for that which we say is with purpose. Our purpose is to prepare them for the GREATER PART -- that they might enter this training School now prepared for them. It is only the beginning of their enlightenment, although there are more places wherein they are to go for yet greater learning, they first prepare within this School, that they might be accepted into the higher one.

Now I bring the word unto mankind at this time, that they be prepared to enter this one which I am now speaking of, for this is the one of greatest concern to us at this hour/time. For it is that which is the place wherein ones are prepared for the next place. In other words, it is this place wherein they earn their passport for the higher place.

There are ones which enter the first, which shall be as the shepherds which have had great training. These shall be as the ones blest, for they shall be as the first to go into the higher School -- for they have given of themself unto their training, for their passport is assured them. Yet they shall be as the monitors unto others which have not known of our part which we have planned for them.

There are ones which shall rejoice to know of our concern for them and the plan for their ongoing learning. These ones shall answer Mine call now. Some shall say "Wait -- see." These shall question and wait (we are in no hurry). Yet, let it be said it is the better part of wisdom to Come <u>Now</u>! For it is foreseen the time is short. We know not how for we only know that which we see. We, the monitors, wait for their preparation. As they prepare themself, they are brought in. There is a season for each one -- a time of fulfillment within the place wherein they now abide. For this do we say, "The time is short -- why wait?" Which ones know how short the time?

Have we not said many times, as ye are prepared so shall ye receive? Now we say, when ye are sufficiently prepared for to enter this School, We of the "Host" shall be fully prepared to welcome thee/ or them as one in "Fellowship". This is the beginning of thine awakening -- <u>just the beginning</u>. Why tell thee more at this time?

* * * * *

Sori Sori: This I would do. It would profit thee to give thine time unto Me for this project. It shall take priority at this time, for it is expedient that this part go with the other portion or part. Let us now finish this appendix unto the second section or part of this book, which shall be called "The Intercom Messages from the Higher Planes." Go not forth from thy place of abode within the next few days in which we shall do this work. Rest thine pore -- for the morrow cometh quickly.

* * * * *

Sori Sori: Give unto them as I give unto thee these words. For they are Mine responsibility. It is thine responsibility to receive of Me correctly and give it unto them as I have given unto thee. Yet I say it shall not go forth from Mine hand imperfect. This shall be as I have said it -- no embellishment. Nothing which is of darkness shall touch these Mine documents, for I have a Plan -- a perfect plan for them. No man shall find himself capable of improving on Mine plan.

Yet I see them waiting to criticize, and tear apart that which I am preparing for them. They cannot know Mine plan, for it is not as yet revealed unto them. The part which I give unto thee, Mine handmaiden, shall be included within these words which I am causing to be written for the good of all. This is no small part of Mine Plan. Let no man think himself so wise that he can be unto Me critic. The time is come when I shall give unto many a portion - - each unto his preparation and unto his fortune. There is a portion for each one which I have called as Mine servant -- for that which he is prepared to do. Some are as ones timid - - fearful, and therefore not prepared to go all the way with Me. Others are fearless and they step out upon the water with Me. They question not the plan.

I hear some question: "What is the Plan?" I say unto them, and for their sake I say it, be ye as ones patient and ye shall see -- for it is the

84

better part of wisdom that ye wait while following Me. Yet, unto them which choose to criticize Me, the Lord God, I say unto them, O ye foolish children; wherein have ye been prepared to speak of Me as an underling -- when I have brought thee forth as one alive and given unto thee that which hast been thine just reward? For as ye have sown, ye reap. To the ones which have sown to the wind, they reap the whirlwind. Dost thou, Mine children, know that which I am saying unto thee? Study well these Mine words, for they are designed to serve well Mine purpose.

I shall define again, lest thou hast forgotten that which I have given unto thee. Mine purpose is: To bring thee out of bondage that ye suffer no more. Yet, ye shall be as one which hast the mind to receive Me, and of Me.

Give unto Me credit for knowing that which I am about, and come unto me as a little child -- humble, unopinionated, and clean of hands, with a pure heart. For none shall enter into Mine place of abode with unclean hands and a heart which is hardened with all sorts of bigotry, shame, and unjust condemnation.

When it is expedient that I speak unto the children of Earth, I find one which is of a mind to give unto the populace that which is good and profitable unto the ones in need. I give as the need is of the greatest concern. I give as I see fit, for I know that which I am about.

While I give unto some in greater depth -- stronger measure -- stronger meat that they might be prepared to follow where I lead them -- yea, I have a Plan which shall not fail Mine purpose. These ones which have the will to follow Me shall be as ones prepared to go into the place wherein there is but the Light which never fails. The glory of it!

As for the ones which will to give themself the bitter cup, they shall drink deeply of it. They shall come to know they have betrayed themself. For this I am come, that All might awaken and return unto their rightful estate -- the place prepared for the righteous. Know ye what that word means? I have caused it to be defined herein. Have ye noticed it? Or wast ye sleeping? This word, "Right use of the law of Life," which is that of the Christ -- pure.

Hast thou considered honestly that which ye do -- that which ye have caused to be done? Hast thou given unto the sick comfort, to the hungry bread -- or hast thou given unto them a stone?

Hast ye put thine finger upon the scale when they give the penny for the loaf? Hast thou put sand in the meal, the flour? Hast thou put thine hand in their pocket?

Hast thou given unto thy dog bread, while thy neighbor's child cries for bread? Hast thou brought shame upon thine household?

Be ye blest to answer "No" honestly. Think not to deceive Me! For I see thee as thou art -- not as ye perceive thine self. For unto the unclean I say, I see that ye are as ones puffed up in thine self-conceit. Thine ego is black -- I say black, tainted. It is a stench unto the clean of heart -- the pure of heart. I see the ones which are the impure -- which are filled with all sorts of iniquity,

Know ye this meaning? I suggest ye ponder this meaning. It would profit thee much. I see thee as a hypocrite -- making excuses for thine deeds which are cause of guilt which follows thee and causes thee shame. Be ye one to think -- ponder -- meditate upon these, Mine words. Take ye heed, for the day of accounting is upon thee!

I would speak unto the glutton -- the one which gives no thought of his Benefactors, while he gorges himself on the carcass of the carrion -- eats and runs -- thoughtless of the hungry ones which are crying for bread. I see them as ones heedless of them which have no place to lay their head, the ones which freeze to death.

Let Me ask of them of which I speak am speaking: What hast thou done to give them relief? What hast thou given unto thy society in which ye reside? Hast thou put a penny in the pot? Hast thou petitioned the politician? Hast thou raised thine voice in wisdom and concern for better understanding - improvement of or for thine brothers in dire need? Hast thou stopt to speak unto these downtrodden, sodden ones which languish in thy public places, dejected and forgotten?

While I speak unto the ones which are thusly concerned with these I have spoken of, ye shall be as ones filled with love for all mankind, sincerity. Let not it be for praise or recognition of thine fellow man. Let compassion be within thee. Give unto them no condemnation -- no cause for pain. Judge them not, for ye know not that which they are! Ye, too, hast been both drunkard -- whoremonger -- thief -- murderer -- all these things ye are guilty of. Ye have carried that guilt with thee for many long cycles of time. Now I say, the time is come when ye shall find that which ye have hidden from thine own self. Bring it out, lest it haunt thee.

This is much to ponder. Yet it is just a puny morsel for thine mind to dwell upon, that ye be as one to face thine own record which ye have written upon the Akasia, which ye shall read. Yea, ye shall stand before thine own self -- and see thine self as ye are in truth -- in thine totality. Ye shall see as ye read that which ye have recorded within or upon these records.

Be ye blest to read and answer for thine own self. While there shall be the ones which stand with thee to bear witness of thee, these shall be as the recorders -- the ones have been thine Benefactors. For they are part of the court of justice, which ye know not.

Let us consider these things in the Light of the Radiant One -- which holds the plan of redemption in His hand.

* * * * *

Sori Sori: By Mine own hand shall ye be blest to give unto them which ask of thee thine blessings. Have I not given unto them as I have given unto thee? Art we not one -- even as I am one with Mine Father?

We are one -- one of spirit -- one of intention, even as the Father-Son relation. He hast given unto Me Being, and I have given unto thee Being. Even so, we are one with the All -- the totality of the All.

There is naught to give or to take away from the totality, is there? For the All is the everything, which exists on all planes in all places and throughout the Cosmos -- which makes us one with the All. All things which exist are kin -- be it snail or panther, in the world of man. God or man, all are kin -- by virtue of life which is the whole -- which ye have been prone to think separate, and of no concern unto thee.

O, Mine beloved ones, thou hast walked blindly. Ye have not known the fullness of thine inheritance. Ye have grabbed at straws while ye have green pasture in which to explore! I say unto thee this day, Come - Come -- Abide with Me and we shall be as "One".

Shall I tell thee again that which ye do is because of the Life which is given unto thee through or by our Father's Grace? Let us give unto Him the praise -- His is the Glory- the Power is His! Yet he hast endowed unto us all that He Is -- worlds without end.

Be ye as one with Him. Feel the Love, the Life, and give thanks. Rejoice that He hast sent unto thee ones which know that which is One with Him. These are thy Benefactors. The difference 'tween them and thine self is -- they know them self to Be -- while it is hidden from thee.

Now the time is come when ye shall awaken unto that which hast sustained thee while thou hast dreamed thine dreams of illusion. The season of awakening is upon thee. Now this is the time of awakening -- the blossoming time of the Soul when ye shall lift up thine eye and see that which ye are. And ye shall rejoice with Me, for I am the One Sent to bring thee home. I offer the living water. Ye shall choose it or reject it, as ye will. There shall be a place prepared to receive each one -- as their part of their own creation -- that which they have put within their "bank" or barn, they shall claim for their own, as their harvest.

Know ye what that means -- "thine harvest"? It means that which ye have sown, ye shall find it hast taken root and matured for thine reaping: Art thou prepared to gather in thine harvest? It is thine! Thou hast given unto it thine strength and attention. Thou shall father thine child and take full responsibility of thine part of the reaping. For each and every one hast his share meted out unto him in this harvest season. The sowing -- then cometh the season of blooming -- seeding -- and then the <u>great</u> gathering-in. Now is the day of gathering-in. What shall it be?

* * * * *

Sori Sori: It is for the generations to come that this word which I shall give unto thee this day shall be prepared now. For the past generation, or this present one, shall not understand Mine word. This which I say within this document is from the School of higher knowledge. Therefore, I say it is for the generation yet unborn.

There shall come upon the Earth a generation which shall walk as "Man". Yet they shall be "<u>Light Beings</u>", born of the Light. These shall not be as ones born of woman. They shall be fully prepared for to be creators, one with the "Source of Being". They are as ones within the womb of Light, <u>now</u> awaiting the call, "<u>Come Forth</u>." These are not asleep as the Earth child, or inhabitants of Earth. These shall bring forth such beings as hast never been upon this planet. They have not known what man of Earth calls "death". These are what is known within Mine place of abode as the "first-born." This is unknown unto the uninitiated -- for it hast never been revealed unto humankind, for he hast been in darkness since he went out for to experience the darkness.

Now, I say the next generation shall learn that there are wondrous things which this one hast not learned or known. They shall see this one as the "Dark Age". So shall it be a proper evaluation. So quickly shall it come to pass, that in the twinkling of an eye it shall be. This shall be as the dawn of the "Golden Age", which hast not been understood in this present day. Let it be understood that which I am saying. The "Golden Age" is that of Great Light -- which shall overcome all negativity -- wherein there is no sorrow -- no suffering. No war shall there be. For the Earth shall be as one purified, and justified. Therefore, no darkness shall be her part -- her heritage. For she shall be a living, shining Light within her new berth, wherein she shall rest in peace.

Blest shall she be -- for long has she suffered -- even as human. Now it is written that there shall be great changes. So it shall be -- as it is written. Too, it is said, "Change is good." Let it be well with thee -- for that have I spoken thusly. For this have I spoken that ye be as one prepared for such changes which shall come about.

Shall I tell thee more? Art thou listening? Dost thou understand Me -- Mine intent -- Mine love for thee? Why do I speak thusly at this time? Dost thou care? Or do ye will to know more?

I say I am come that ye know that which goes on in the "Realm of Light". For this is thine gift of the Father -- given freely that ye be prepared to return unto Him -- thine rightful place of abode.

* * * * *

Beloved of Mine Being: I am come unto thee that I might pay homage unto all which hast labored long in the field of service unto the Father-Mother God. Too, unto Mother Earth. There are ones which have given their life for her, the Earth Mother, that all might be blest of her bounty -- her life. For she hast labored long -- untold cycles for to give footing unto a wayward generation.

Now she shall throw them off and be free of them which we see as laggards. No longer shall she suffer their indignities -- thoughtless of her -- pollute her life streams -- torment her -- waste her provisions -- shame her -- make waste her land and pilfer her choice treasure -- without thought or thanks. By her Grace hast thou been fed and clothed!

91

Hast thou, O thoughtless ones, taken heed? Bless her, as I have given unto thee cause to take thought of her. I have caused the desert to bloom -- the rivers to dry up - - the mountains to tremble -- the skies to belch forth fire. The Earth shall shake and quake, and ye shall run to hide. Yet ye shall find no hiding place -- for this is the day of accounting. Hast thou heard Me say that before? Yea, many times it is said.

Ye have run to and fro -- forgetful of Mine preachments. Ye hast been as ones heedless of the signs I have manifested before thine eyes.

Wherein have ye slept while seeing these manifested before thee? Hast thou wondered from whence cometh these "signs" and wonders? By Mine own hand, Mine children -- by Mine own hand these wonders hast been caused. Look and see. Ye shall be caused to see. Stop and look -- even enjoy them -- and give thanks unto the Father that thou art here to enjoy the great wonders of the changes which are now going on -- all about thee.

While thou hast slept, many things hast occurred, which is forerunner of the great and wondrous moment of the change, which shall happen within the twinkling of an eye. I tell unto thee that which is wise and prudent.

Too, I say unto all, fear naught -- be ye as one prepared. For them which have heard that which I have said and given unto Me their hand, I shall deliver thee out and naught shall harm thee. Nothing of darkness/ evil shall touch thee. Be ye blest to be alert and watchful. Call on Me and I shall hear thee. Yet ye shall not make mock of Me - neither Mine word. Ye shall first love Me -- know that which I am, for there is no deceit within Me. I know thee and thine intent. For this art thou heard -- and answered. Ye are answered in the likeness of thine intent.

Unto the foolish -- they are answered by the foolish - the unknowing ones. Ofttimes the unknowing ones come in disguise, that ye be deceived. Now it is plainly written, "Ye shall come unto me with a pure heart and clean hands." Then I shall take heed of thine call.

Let this suffice as a reminder unto thee of that which hast been written. So be it. I shall give unto thee signs -- yea, reminders, lest ye forget. For I am not about to let ye forget, Mine little ones!

* * * * *

Sori Sori: With the power invested within Me, I say unto thee there shall come upon the Earth a great wave of Light which shall herald the New Age that hast come. For this hast been that which is spoken of in the "olden time". Yet none hast known the meaning of this message unto mankind. This shall occur as the clap of great thunder. It shall roll, and quake the planet Earth. None shall know that which We of the Host are doing, and there shall be great fright and confusion. Yet it hast been said, "Fear naught" -- for We of the Host shall draw nigh unto the Earth. There shall be a host of angelic beings to attend thee. These shall be Mine assistants, which come of their own free will to assist the rescue or lifting up -- which hast been referred to as the "Resurrection". There hast been many which have asked, "What is this?" They have had no revelation upon the subject.

I now say unto thee, and all which are within and upon the planet Earth, "The Resurrection" is the time of rapture -- when Earth man shall be lifted up and rescued from that which the planet shall experience -- such as the Earth shall suffer during her birthing. When she is free of pain, and the Son is born and the after-birth hast been severed from her, she shall be prepared to receive the "Sons of God". For she shall be as

93

the Light of the Sun -- cleansed, fresh and pristine pure -- pure of all contamination. No taint of blood shall be upon her.

Yet her offspring shall have some resemblance of the Mother and the taint shall be reflected in it -- her offspring. Therefore, there shall be the place which shall be the home or school for the laggards -- wherein they shall have their memory blanked from them. There shall be the ones which have betrayed themself. They shall begin from the beginning, even as the primitive Earthman. They shall be in total blankness -- no memory of past existence, of being. Many shall be as ones sad to behold, bent with sorrow and hatred, and all sorts of inherited sorrow. They shall wonder of their plight and cry out for Light -- while knowing not that which it is or how to find it. Pity shall they be.

Yet they shall be as ones remembered -- and monitored for their progress. As they learn the lesson of life -- the laws of life -- they, too, shall be brought out of their place which they have fortuned unto themself the "lesser part." For none are left alone. They are within the "All" -- therefore, they are the wards of the Sons of God, which shall be unto them Benefactors. There shall be love and justice for All.

* * * * *

Sori Sori: These which shall go into their strange and new place shall be as the sleepers, which are unaware that they are moved into another place. They shall awaken and find that they have no memory of past existence. Then they shall dream strange dreams which they do not understand. They shall be confused, for their surroundings shall seem strange, and wonder of it shall fill them. There shall be a foreboding of their future -- and fear and anxiety shall be within them -- and loneliness shall be their lot. A longing shall they have, for some faint memory shall haunt them.

This shall be the lot of the ones which hast not alerted themself -- the traitors. They shall know all sorts of discomfort and sadness. For it is said, and truly it is so, as ye sow so shall ye reap. Like unto that which is sown - so the reaping. Be it wheat or brambles.

* * * * *

Sori Sori: Ye shall give unto them which shall read this little book this word which I shall give unto thee for them. It is with greatest love and respect at this time. I am one of the Host. I come from a great distance, that I might stand as one with mine fellow brothers at this auspicious occasion -- that of the birthing.

Each of us add our love and blessing. For it is now come when the little red star shall find her new berth, and she shall move out as one guided and cared for, and in great Light shall she be moved. There is no pen or tongue that could give unto thee one inkling of such an operation. The wonder of it fills us with joy! Yet it is not the first birthing that we have attended.

Could ye but see from our point of view the preparation for this occasion, ye should not survive the power and glory of it. There shall be such power released, that it would be impossible for a hu-man in flesh to survive it.

These ones which shall be put on the new place shall be in deep sleep. They shall have no knowledge of how they came to be there. It shall be a great mystery -- which shall not be revealed unto them until they have awakened.

95

This is likened unto that of the present population of Earth. Have they, too, not betrayed themself? Are they, too, not part of Earth mankind? Is it not said that this is the day of sifting and sorting? "Some shall be taken -- some shall be left." So be it there are ones which shall remember who they are -- their Source -- and be aware of their many embodiments -- be it on Earth or many other planets. The population, for the most part, hast slept that long, deep sleep -- knowing not their heritage.

Now it is of great concern unto us that this Plan be brought to a fruitful conclusion. We are prepared for this mission -- the Light of the Eternal One. By the combined knowledge, we as one power -- oneness of purpose -- shall bring the "Mother" into her new berth safely. Could ye image such a mission? We stand in awe of the majesty of it!

Be it so that we come for the good of all -- for the All is One -- one body ensouled in our Father Eternal. Be it so that there are untold numbers of parts and entities within the "One". "We" move in concert -- as one -- one mind -- one purpose. There is no quibbling over, or about missions -- place -- status - methods, etc. -- among us -- with us. We are the enlightened of the "All" Father God -- timeless -- endless -- tireless He is. He Is The Light in which ye and I art ensouled. This makes of us All One in Him.

Therefore, when one of the universes with their many stars-planets are in need, we give of our love and assistance. Let it be understood that there is no separation within Creation. All things art bound together by Father's love. Ye know not such love.

Ye of the world of man hast abused and misused the word "Love". Ye are yet in darkness. Ye dreamers are now on the threshold of thine awakening. What a glad day it is! Be ye blest this day by this great company -- the Mighty Host.

I am one of the Starship.

* * * * *

Sori Sori: Make way -- for it is now come when many shall go into their new place prepared -- or unprepared. For there is necessity that it be so.

While each shall be accounted for, not one shall be lost from Mine sight. It shall be as great sorrow and shock for the child of Earth. It is said that no man knoweth the hour -- that his number shall be called. It is so. So be it.

While it, too, is said that "it is wisdom to know" -- know what? ye ask. Hast thou not heard Me? That ye may not be caught off guard - unaware.

It is said, <u>Fear not</u>. Yet I see thee, ye heedless ones, yet running -- looking for physical comforts. Dost thou think I am playing games, such as the magician? Pity are they which give unto themself the bitter cup.

Hast it not been written that this is the last call? 'Tis so! This is the day of decision. Be ye wise, and get on with thine preparation -- for this I wait. For it is the Father's Will that ye be prepared to return unto Him with Me.

Give ye heed unto Mine word. For I have gone the long way to prepare for thine homecoming. Each and every one shall have that which they have earned. What shall be thine share?

Be ye not so foolish as to sell thine inheritance for poor counterfeit penny. Blest art they which are prepared to return home with Me.

I hear the laggard say: "O, I have heard that stuff -- I'm sick of it." Yea, ye shall be filled with fear -- knowing not which way to run -- filled with remorse. For Mine words shall return to haunt thee. While I am sent to Earth that there be no one overlooked, therein is justice and mercy. For We of the Host shall find thee by thine Light. Dost thou have one? Is it sufficient? I pray so!

Dost a man go out into the pit of blackness to find the laggard, while there are ones waiting with Light shining brightly? I might use one of thy platitudes: "First come, first served."

* * * * *

Sori Sori: There is no time to lose. Yet there is wisdom in taking time -- to learn well that which "We" bring unto thee, or present unto thee. There art many times that we speak unto the ones which are as ones willing to be brought in. Yet they give unto us no ear. They talk -- talk -- thinking themself wise. They are as children playing games. With their prattling they reveal their foolishness. They close us out; therefore, they know not that which we have for them. These are ones which find a crumb and cry, I have found -- I know. Yet they have but the crumb -- they are ones satisfied. Even so, they make such confusion as to invite the enemy in.

Now I say, the ones which pick up the crumb and rush out crying, "Look! Look! See that which I have -- Come partake with Me" -- these are ones which think themself wise. They are satisfied with the crumb, while we bring the loaf. We have called unto them also -- Come to the feast! They are too busy going hither and yon with the crumb. I ask of them: Prepare thine self for greater -- greater and stronger food -- which shall enrich thine soul -- and make ready thine self for the banquet.

Be ye as one to hear Mine call, for I shall be as one prepared to receive thee into the chambers of greater learning. Hast thou heard Mine call? Received Mine invitation to the feast? Blest art they which have accepted the invitation, for it is the Last Call.

* * * * *

Sori Sori: Be ye as one which hast heard Mine voice -- felt Mine touch -- and given unto Me thine hand. And I shall be unto thee all that ye have need of. For I am not limited. I am one with the Source of All Being. So be it I am prepared to bring thee out. Give unto Me credit for being that which I Am.

It is now come when We of the Host hast prepared this place wherein We shall receive thee. Be ye blest to come forth as one prepared.

* * * * *

Sori Sori: It is now come that the School of which I have spoken is ready to receive the candidates. By this I mean that it is now open unto the ones which are prepared to enter in. There shall be ones which have refused Mine invitation. These shall be as ones which shall be the sleepers -- while there shall be many that come prepared to enter.

Now, for the first time I shall speak of the work which shall be done within this School. It shall be for the purpose of bringing yet others out of bondage -- even as the first which hast come. As the first is prepared,

99

they shall go out as shepherds -- to find the newly awakened. These shall be trust-worth and responsible for their part.

There shall be great Light within them, and they shall be called as the "chosen" to go unto the next one to be brought in as their monitors and brothers/sisters -- even as the first were sent out from the place wherein I am.

There shall be no laggards within this place. This is the place carefully screened. There are no mistakes in our Plan. While it is but the "New School", we which hast brought it into being know that which we are about. For this do we say that ye which are fortuned to enter shall be in "good hands", for long have we been at this preparation. It gives us much joy to announce that it is now open.

Thus, it shall be as nothing imagined by the uninitiated. For there hast been many enlightened ones which hast had a part in the preparation of this said School. When one enters herein, they shall be filled with awe and joy -- for they shall know that they have been as one chosen. They shall be as one glad! And they shall be filled with thanksgiving. Too, they shall be glad to go unto the next in line -- to be unto them monitors, even as they received -- even unknowingly. This shall be, as ye shall find thine passport into the higher learning.

Hast thou heard that which I have been saying in these documents? Or hast thou been napping? Should that be So, I suggest ye look again! For there are great truths -- nuggets of purest gold hidden within these Mine words. Be ye not hasty to discard them, for they art designed for the one which hast the WILL to be brought out and prepared to serve in such capacity for the good of all.

Now, as I have given unto thee this much, ye shall accept it or reject it, as ye will. For it is not our intent to bring the sleepers in. It is our intent to awaken them unto their inheritance -- to bring them home. It is our part to enlighten the ones which are "prepared" to enter into this School. Shall ye be as one ready for thine call? It is said herein that thine name shall be called. Shall ye remember? Shall ye answer?

Ye which answer shall be given a number and a "new name", which ye shall accept with great joy -- for ye shall know ye have earned it! Praise unto the Father-Mother God for His mercy and love.

Now we shall bring forth great Light -- which shall be thy shield and buckler -- and nothing of darkness shall touch thee. For ye are now as one arrayed in Light -- of Mine Light -- for ye have proven thine self as one prepared to wear the Crown of Victory.

Hast thou been as one which hast called Me false? Or an impostor? So be it when ye think thine self wise, I should remind thee again of the traitor which is found by the wayside, crying in despair. There, alone in his aloneness, he cries out unto "his god" for help. Let it be so. While it is so, his call shall be heard also. Yet, he shall, too, be subject to the same law as ye and I, Mine dear ones -- even as ye and I.

We would have thee consider well Mine invitation unto the banquet -- for the table is set. Is thine place set? I say unto thee, ye write thine own place card -- by the will to go all the way with Me.

I ask not lip service, for I see not that which ye say. I see thine intent -- that which ye are -- that which lies buried within.

So be it, it is written, Ye shall clean out all the darkness -- foulness -- conceit -- hatred -- jealousy -- hypocrisy -- selfishness -- which is that which shall be unto thee thine burden which ye cannot bring with thee. Art thou prepared to lay them down for thy freedom? -- Art thou ready to leave behind thine "choice possessions"? Yea, friends -- family? I ask thee. Choose ye wisely -- then give unto Me answer. Yet I say I know without thine spoken word -- while ye shall be as one true unto thine own self, for nothing is hidden within the Light of the Living Christ, which I Am.

* * * * *

Sori Sori: Wherein is it written, "There shall be ones which walk the Earth which have not been born of woman"? These are ones sent from the place wherein I am. These are of the Father sent -- sent for the purpose which shall be unknown unto the uninitiated. For it is of great concern that man of flesh hast the temper which is curious to the degree of evil intent.

Theirs (these of the Father sent) is the part which shall be a "<u>secret mission</u>", and no man dare to claim to be one of these. For none shall mimic one of these sent of the Father -- for the law is sure and swift.

By the word shall he be made manifest upon the Earth. He shall need no place to lay his head, no pillow for his head, no food from thy table -- for he shall be free. No thing shall he need, for he is self sufficient.

While He is but a thought away, He shall be every place where there is "work" to do. He shall bring much Light to the ones within the governments of the Earth. There shall be great changes, which shall be for the good of all. While the populace sleeps He shall give forth great plans, and the ones which are alert -- with the will to serve the Light --

shall arise themself and make known their intention. Then He, which is the one assigned unto the part of bringing greater understanding unto all the people, shall be as the unseen cause of this onrush of Light.

It shall be as no man hast seen. This shall be the "end time" manifestation, which causes much confusion and suffering. Yet many shall be removed, that the greater part be made manifest. While the populace shall cry, "Where is there justice in this?" they but see with clouded vision -- knowing not that there is wisdom and justice in a Plan they know not.

It is written that heads of governments shall fall -- and Light shall there be. This is the "end time" spoken in thy books of old -- when thine streets shall be filled with blood.

Hast thou waited for more signs? Or hast thou slept thru these signs? Do ye wait for more? Can ye not see that which goes on about thee?

I say unto thee, "This is the day of awakening." Yet there is the Host which is in its place, prepared to descend upon the Earth when the hour cometh for this to be known unto man. While these art now among thee, it is but the foregoing preparation for the Host.

Think ye that this is but a day of needless struggle? I say unto thee, it is the greatest of all jobs -- one for the Host -- which stands ready to make its self known unto the world of man. It is said: "O man of Earth, arise from thy stupor and be ye aware of that which goes on about thee." Then ye shall clean out thine own closet and make clean thine own house. Clean out that which ye have hidden therein unknowingly -- yea, even unto that which haunts thee. Forgive thineself thine unknowing, and stand as one within the Light which is the cause of thine being.

First, ye shall be as one willing to do that which I shall ask of thee. Ye shall lay down all thine preconceived ideas of ME, the Lord of Lords, the Prince of Peace. Thine Benefactor I am. I am come that there be peace, yet it is said, "I bring not peace," For it is the law I cannot give that which is thine. It is Mine part to <u>direct</u> thee -- while it is thine to follow Mine directions and Plan.

I do have a great Plan. Yet ye have not prepared thine self for the fullness of it. "We" make no pretense of the Plan. We of the Host are of the Father sent -- with the fullness of this plan of which I am speaking. Ye, the ones which I am addressing now, are but stirring -- I might say, for thine sake, with one eye open.

While I/We are doing our part, ye are as ones playing games -- yea, "games" -- even within the so-called "houses of worship". Let it be said here that it goes on record within these documents, that the hypocrisy and brazen subterfuge shall be exposed unto the Light. Forget not that which I have said -- or given unto thee as a reminder. For every word of deceit or misused power shall haunt thee -- follow thee, until it is cleaned out -- transmuted. Hear ye Me in this, for it shall profit thee!

By Mine own hand I have penned this, Mine word. Make way, for the time is at hand when ye shall stand before thine own self in self-examination. Ye shall receive that which ye have justly earned. Have ye heard that aforehand? Hast thou believed? What hast thou done to redeem thyself?

Be not so foolish as to think ye can give thine own responsibility unto Me, for there is no such law that I take the responsibility unto Mine self. Therefore, I say again, "Alert thine self." Be up and about thine "house cleaning". Make straight the way for Mine coming, that I might enter into thine house and sup with thee. So let it be well with thee.

* * * * *

Sori Sori: I am speaking now of the ones which are alert unto Mine presence. These shall understand that which I say unto them. Therefore, I shall give unto them in greater measure -- stronger meat and drink -- and they shall not become drunken or puffed up.

So be it, their part shall be as sealed from the eyes of the wicked or unknowing ones which would but be as the destroyers. These are the Anti-Christs -- which would, were it possible, destroy our Plan -- Our mission. They would abort it. Know ye these ones? Hast they not been at thine door? Hast they not given unto thee the bitter cup?

Now I say unto thee again, thou hast kept thine peace and "fought a good fight". Thou hast been true unto thine trust. Ye have been as one which hast obeyed each commandment. Each precept which hast been given, ye have taken unto thineself. Now ye shall see that which hast been accomplished with thine effort and loyalty unto the service of the Father-Mother God. Thine time is come when ye shall be brought in, and this shall be the day for which ye have waited. So be it and Selah.

* * * * *

Sori Sori: Wherein is it written that there shall be great sorrow? When hast there been no sorrow? Hast thou noticed? Now it is come when the populace shall come to know that which is said unto them for the

105

purpose of alerting them -- preparing them for that which shall come upon them.

They which shall cry "prophets of doom" shall give some thought unto their laughter, for soon it shall turn into "tears". Think ye We of the higher realms, understanding the greater view, are eager to be the ones to give this alarm -- to distress and bring fear to thine hearts? Nay, Mine blessed one! For it is with great effort and compassion that we labor long to prevent thy suffering and fear.

Is it not compassion that we give unto thee of our vision? Know ye that We of the Host of thine Benefactors are better equipped to see/learn that which shall come upon the Earth than thy most learned scientists -- with their greatest of equipment? For have "We" not been their teachers -- "inspirators" for such as they have accepted, and even boasted of, as being of their very own?

While we receive long aforehand that knowledge, and pass it on unto the ones which are listening, this we do constantly -- with great knowledge of thy needs. When one is prepared to receive such inspiration, then one oversees the project until it is brought unto its completion, for the good of mankind.

Not always is it used for the good of All, we are very sorry to say. We are no respecter of persons. We "work" for the "good of all". Yet that which we release from our hands/minds unto thine own is ofttimes misused. This shall cease, Mine loved ones! For we shall find a way of screening and protecting our part -- that which we place within the hands of the Earth scientists. For they which are tried and tested -- found worthy to give these visions to -- shall be protected. And the ones which have the intent to destroy -- misuse -- and pilfer, shall be dealt with in such a manner that they cannot misuse that which the Benefactors have brought about -- be they Space Brothers or of the Earth.

Let it be understood that we are well prepared to open up the storehouse of our knowledge when ye of the Earth are prepared for to use Our Blessing for the "good of all".

The traitors -- which receive of our blessing even as the righteous, the innocent ones, then pilfer the proceeds -- misuse it as their own -- shall not prosper. These shall be brought up short! Alas, they shall wonder at their failures. Be ye as ones which have given of thine self in love and wisdom for the good of all, and ye shall have our protection. So be it and Selah. Now, ye shall give this unto any and all which shall receive it. Unto them which reject it, let it be upon their shoulders.

I am one of thine Benefactors Eng

* * * * *

Sori Sori: Give unto Me credit for being that which I am. I am one of the Fleet of the XTX. I am known here by the name of Zampu. This is mine word with thee at this hour. However, we shall have some time together at another time.

Be ye as one to receive me. I shall be brief and considerate of conditions about thee. I shall make no demands of thee. Yet we shall be as one of purpose. It shall be profitable unto our mission -- yours and mine. Be ye blest to receive me, for I come in love and Light of our Commander. It is with his blessing that I come. So be it and Selah.

* * * * *

Sori Sori: There is but one which is the source of thine Life -- the Source, which is the one from which All blessings flow. Unto "Him" ("It") give thanks. For from Him, within Him, thou hast thine existence. Thou art One with It - Life of his Life -- for He is just that. He gives, and He takes -- for All is His. He is without gender -- neither male nor female. He is All that is -- therefore, He can speak any tongue.

For hast He not given unto thee voice? Hast He not given unto thee eyes to see -- and power to put out thine hand to touch the rose? Why art thou so thoughtless, my little ones, of that which ye are? Art thou not One with Him?

Hast He not been unto thee the Father-Mother? Where think ye ye came from? Where think ye are going? Have ye given thought unto these things I speak of? Why art thou so fearful and restless?

For thine sake I call thine attention unto that which ye remember not. Once, in times without number, ye were within a place wherein there existed naught of darkness -- only pristine purity. Time was, when of thine own will ye chose to go out from that place for to explore into the unknown. This for thine own pleasure -- call it curiosity if ye will. Yet ye cannot comprehend that which I am giving unto thee in simplest terms possible -- even as thine "Genesis" was written. This is but a reminder that ye did not have thine beginning upon the little orb of Earth -- not as thy memory recalls, even as it is written,

Hast thou remembered that recorded story? Why should I tell thee of thine beginning? Could ye comprehend? Nay, just as ye have no memory of thine birth in flesh -- or are ye one of them which remember? Blest art they which do remember, for it shall be as part of their awakening.

Let us speak of the memory. Is it not a record? Is it not for the most part sealed up? Why? Did ye not agree to that when ye agreed to come into this state of being upon this planet? Why? For the reason that this planet, Earth, is the testing planet -- a school for to hone and quicken the child of the firmaments.

Know ye that ye are wanderers? Yea, wanderers! Long hast thou wandered thru the many cycles, and other, many other planets hast given thee footing. Yet it hast been said, "Ye are creatures of the air." Know ye this?

I say unto thee there is nothing that shall be hidden from thee when thou art prepared to receive thine inheritance. <u>Ye shall awaken</u>! For this am I come -- let it be as the Father hast willed.

* * * * *

Sori Sori: What think ye is meant by "prepare"? What think ye is meant by "Give thine self unto Me"?

Let it be understood that one shall, and must change his willful way -- which is unbecoming unto a Light Being. For within the place wherein they are is but purity of thought -- naught to mar their part, or atmosphere. There is but love and peace.

To give thine self unto Me, I say, none come unto Me against his will, none come unclean. These are the ones which shall find their own place, which they have earned. They shall be in their own environment -- be it peace or war, Light or darkness.

* * * * *

Sori Sori: For this hour let us consider them which are called into Mine service. Now say unto them as I would say unto them. They shall walk as one which hast answered Mine call. They shall walk as ones sober. They shall be as brothers -- filled with love and respect. For this hast they been sibored in the way in which they go, that they might be prepared to enter into the School of higher learning. For this do I speak unto all, for it is foreseen that there shall be peace and poise among Mine servants. Then they shall receive their just reward. And they shall learn the way of the initiate and behold the peace and joy of knowing the Way of Righteousness. This is Mine word at this hour -- let it suffice.

Sananda hast spoken.

* * * * *

Sori Sori: The hour hast struck when thine name is recorded upon the Akasia -- the record complete. Make no mistake about that, for it is correctly recorded that each and every act -- every word -- every thought is recorded therein. This is the word I would give unto thee this day. For thine own sake I give it unto thee. Consider well that which I bring, for it is given unto thee that ye become aware of that which ye do.

Blest art they which create with understanding and love. The word love, as man knows it to be, is an abomination, and that which shall torment thee in the day of accounting. It is with wisdom and love that I remind thee of thine responsibility unto thine own self. For every word and deed is faithfully recorded and weighed. Compare not Mine words unto thine foolish concept of the process of "weighing and sorting". For thou hast not one iota of knowledge of that which I am

110

speaking of. Yet that hast not the slightest difference unto Me, for I know that which I am endeavoring to cause ye, the unknowing ones, to come to know -- that which ye have not been aware of. Yet it is written in many of thine books -- hast thou not found it?

This is one of the wise "<u>live</u>" portions with lessons that ye shall learn -- 'ere ye return unto thine place of going out -- purified and justified. For each word of "damnation" shall be transmuted and atoned for. Know ye this? Art thou mindful of that which goes out from thine mouth? Hast thou been aware of that which ye have created? Know ye that which goes out shall return unto thee threefold, bringing its likeness <u>threefold</u>! Know ye what that means?

Should ye forget, I say take ye "stock". Look -- recount that which ye have done -- said -- and the harvest reapt. Think ye not that which ye have spewed from thine mouth hast escaped the eye of the law! For the Record Keeper is the all-seeing eye.

Nothing escapes Him/It, for it is the One which hast brought thee forth -- and within thee is that which blesses or curses thee. By thine own self thou art blest or cursed. Yea, by thine own action, deed or word. None other shall atone for thine misused energy. None other shall reap thine harvest. None other shall receive thine reward. Even as the deed, so shall the reward be.

* * * * *

Sori Sori: I give these words unto thee that ye shall find them profitable. Let it be. For that have I sent them forth upon our Intercom. I bless thee to receive them -- that they be aware of that which they do. So let it

111

profit all which are in need of wisdom and preparation for their inheritance in full.

* * * * *

Sori Sori: This is Mine word unto the ones which know Me not. I am come that they become aware of Me and Mine mission. For that I am speaking unto them in this manner. I have a Plan whereby they shall be as ones enlightened. They first shall be willing to accept that which I have for them, for I do not force upon them Mine precepts. Not even they are meant to free them from the bonds which holds them bound in darkness and misery.

Could they but see their pitiful plight, they would cry out for Mine assistance. Then I should rush unto their call. By the power which is Mine, willed unto Me of the Father, I say I am the Lord God -- come unto thee for the purpose of giving unto one and all that which the Father hast for them.

He hast that which he hast willed unto thee until thou hast prepared thineself and willed thine return. So be it -- I am the Wayshower. I am the one thru which ye enter into the place of His abode. None enter save through Me -- for I am the Gate through which ye enter.

Be ye not deluded by the dark brothers, which give unto thee sweet honeyed words which ye so love to hear. Ye hast danced to their music and become drunken -- and forgotten thine self-responsibility. These things I should remind thee of, for I know that which ye are and that which ye do. For the greater part, ye have put Me aside -- as of no account. Yet when ye are faced with some great tragedy in which ye are part, and think to escape, ye cry out to Me.

I shall say unto thee, where hast thou been? What hast thou done to bring this upon thine self, Mine child? Did ye not hear Mine call? Did ye not feel Mine hand upon thine shoulder?

Now ye shall account for thine self -- and answer truly that which is asked of thee. Remember that there is nothing hidden from Me. Yet I judge thee not. It is clearly stated that ye art thine own judge according unto the law of the Cosmos. Let it be for the good of all that I speak unto the unknowing, wayward ones, for art they ones to be pitied? Bless them, that they might see the Light.

* * * * *

Sori Sori: By Mine own hand shall these words be penned for thine own sake. I shall cause these things to be brought unto thine attention. So be it that I am the Lord thy God -- Born of Light I Am. Therefore, I am the first born of the "All", Father-Mother God -- brought forth as the "First Born" which I am. Let thine first consideration be of Me -- Mine Plan which is conceived within the realm of Light in which ye and I, have our being.

This is the new day in which many new things shall be revealed unto thee, the children which hast been bound by the dragon. For he hast given unto thee of himself that which he hast devised to ensnare and bind thee. He is the father of deceit and lies. There is no mercy or compassion within him. He hast no love for anything what-so-ever. He contrives ways and means to ensnare the Creator's children -- which are born of Him, the All Light. He, the dragon, sits on the altars set up by man which think themself wise. They compose sweet sonnets to please the ears of them which he holds bound, while he sings to them that which pleases them. They, these which are his slaves, have become

113

drunken on his "sweet wine". They have given ear unto the great lie which they have perpetuated thru ages past.

Now it is come when I shall send unto thee ones which shall awaken thee, and ye shall come to know the truth from the lie -- which ye, man of earth, hast accepted as truth.

I come that ye might know of the truth -- for I am of Mine Father sent that ye be prepared to return unto Him with Me. So let it be as He wills.

* * * * *

Sori Sori: Let us speak of that which binds the unknowing ones. It is with the love for Mine children that I speak of the dark one which conceives these ways and means to bind them -- blind their eyes that they see not his nefarious schemes, the lies which he hast implanted within the mind of man. So be it that the battle for freedom is on, for I say unto thee, Mino children, I am come with a Host of angelic beings which are prepared to set thee free. I ask of thee -- art thou ready to receive of them that which shall be thine knowing? O, the surety of it -- the glad freedom which shall be thine ye have not imaged. So be it we come as "One" -- of one intent -- one of mind which hast been given of the Father-Mother wherein there is no darkness.

* * * * *

Sori Sori: Be ye blest this day -- for this do I come at this hour. Ye shall now say unto them as I would say, that many shall come crying -- asking of thee: How do I become a "member" of this said School? Where is it? How much is it? Who is the head? How long does it take to become an initiate?

114

Let Me say it again, and I shall say it thrice: None enter save by their own effort -- their dedication and of true intent. Each shall be well-qualified; then he shall be found and brought in. Weary not thine self looking for signs/signals or for familiar things as hints or callings, for there shall be none. Is it not truly said: There shall be no signs to suit thine fancies -- to prick thine ego? Let it be said, ye need not imagine thine self worthy to enter, for ye know not. For ye have not as yet had thine memory restored.

* * * * *

Sori Sori: By Mine hand shall I bless thee this day, for there shall be great things done in a very short while. There shall be many brought in and they shall come to know that there is no death. They shall be as ones to learn that there is nothing to fear, for they shall be brought out from the shadow wherein they have been under the black hood.

None shall want or fear, which come into this School of learning. They shall be free from all deception -- all that hast held them in bondage. The shackles shall fall from them, for they shall come to know as We of the Council know. Bless them which come unto thee which shall bring thee in -- for they are first prepared herein. Then they are qualified to fetch thee, for they then know that which they shall do that these brothers be lifted up.

Be ye as one prepared to go all the way with Me. So shall ye be blest as I have been blest. So be it and Selah.

* * * * *

Sori Sori: Many have given of themself, their energy and love that this School be brot into its fullness and readied to receive the candidate.

115

Now they are within their places, and well prepared to receive any and all which qualify to be admitted. These which are so prepared shall be eternally blest!

* * * * *

Sori Sori: The day swiftly approaches when there shall be a great cry go up from the Earth and the population, for the time of deliverance is now come. Who among thee knows the fullness of it? The mountains shall fall -- the rivers shall be misplaced -- the prairies shall become mountains; and the oceans shall be as the misplaced waters. Nothing shall remain in its old place.

There shall be the great Otavans which shall come to the rescue of them which shall be rescued. This hast been referred to as the "Pick-up". Yet ye have not an iota or concept which is meant by this Exodus -- "the time of the Exodus." Thine mind could not conceive of this "chaos". There is no comparison.

While it shall be the beginning of the "Golden Age", it shall begin in chaos. While ye cannot image such conditions, ye shall be as ones informed of the coming event -- the greatest which this little planet hast ever encountered. Know ye that <u>We</u> foresee that which shall come upon it. Be ye not hasty to make thine plans -- neither to deny this, Mine word. For the foolish would not be so brazen.

Listen unto Me, and I shall give unto thee a Plan -- which ye shall accept or reject. It is Mine part to speak of this, that ye be appraised of that which shall be.

Now within the ether are these things written. Events cast their shadow. We of the Cosmos can read as ye read thine weather charts --

116

just as simple unto us, for we are as prepared for such. Be ye as ones to hear us -- for it is for thy sake that we speak of these things. Yet we say unto thee, <u>Be ye not fearful</u>, for there is a Plan. We know our part well. Now we are calling unto the populace of the Earth, "Prepare thine self for that which shall come upon thee." Have ye given thought unto that call? It is for thine own sake that we have gathered in the places wherein we are -- that we be prepared for <u>instant action</u>. In unison we shall move as one, for we await as One man -- One thought -- One purpose -- that of delivering thee out before the great hour of sorrow.

We ask of thee "CO-OPERATION". Be ye alert. Hear our instructions as we give them unto thee individually. Ask not thine friend or neighbor that which he hast been directed to do, for that, indeed, would be the greatest folly. For to do so might be thine own destruction. I say no two shall have the same instruction. It is said, and rightly so, that each shall have an encoded number and a color -- which shall be his <u>very own</u>. Not even ye shall be aware of this number, for it is not as yet revealed unto thee -- for ye are yet in darkness.

For this are we speaking unto thee, one and all, of this School -- which is prepared for to bring the ones in when they have met the requirements. These have been clearly stated within this, Mine document. Should ye have forgotten or have taken no account, please return unto that part and study well that which hast been recorded in the simplest of terms.

This is not the time to quibble over words! Be not so foolish -- for there is much for us, thine Guardians and Benefactors, to do! We are now asking thine cooperation. It is a smaller part than ours -- little it is that we ask of thee! Yet it depends upon thee how well ye are prepared. When one gives himself the bitter cup, he shall drink of it. Yet none shall leave his post to spare the rebellious traitor which hast betrayed himself.

Do ye understand that which I am saying? I cannot speak any simpler -- in any language. Make no mystery of Mine message, for that is <u>not</u> Mine intent.

Recorded by Sister Thedra

PART III

Now let us begin this portion with these words: Blest are they which hear that which I say unto them. They shall be lifted up. There are ones which await the day of "the lift-off," knowing nothing of the meaning of these words.

Let us be more explicit -- for it is not Mine intent to mislead one of Mine blessed children. Therefore, I shall give unto them that which they might understand and profit thereby. While it is not possible to give unto these ones the fullness of the plan, I shall give them a portion which is possible for even the little child to understand.

It is now come when the Earth has come into her maturity. There is a place prepared for her within the firmaments which shall be her new berth. Now it is come that she shall bring forth a new portion of her body -- even as an earth mother brings forth her "son", which be of great pain. This birth shall not be without great pain, for she shall reel and roll, and in this she shall be guided and directed with loving care by the Ones which are capable of such maneuvers.

For long hast they, these Creators, these Mentors -- which have brought from out the firmaments planets unknown unto man of earth -- they have guided great, huge meteors on their course. These are what ye might call the "Cosmic Midwife", for such they are.

This is the birthing of a man for/by Mother Earth. As she is gently and lovingly guided out of her present bed orbit, she shall give forth this body which she now carries within her womb. As she goes out into a place appropriate, she shall give forth/release the after-birth. Now this son shall be a full-grown new moon -- a moon which shall be smaller than the present moon -- while the present moon shall be as the older brother unto the new one.

Now, the after-birth -- shall we call it that, or such for the sake of Mine tale; this after-birth shall be as an undeveloped moon, smaller in size, and it shall need much care and developing. Thereby it shall come into its adolescence within the time allotted such things. Then it shall become a glory to behold within a short time. How long -- it is not yet calculated in man's time/earth time.

This is part of the great changes that are to come about. We have been speaking of these, yet it is not possible to get these which are asleep to understand a minute portion of such changes. The cosmogony of the firmaments are yet a mystery unto them. While we are speaking of these great cosmic changes, we of necessity must use language such as can be understood by the multitude -- such as hast been used through thine history.

This is that for which the School I am speaking of hast been brought forth, that all which have the will to learn might be able to learn of these marvelous wonders, of Creator's works. These are the things We of the Mighty Council would have each and every one know.

So be it. For this have we labored, that none are left in darkness. For this do we reach our hand unto thee and say "Come." Let it be for the good of all mankind do we call, "Come ye out from among them" which will to come. Be ye as ones willing, and a thing apart. Be as one which can walk tall -- stand on thine own feet -- as one which stands up to be counted. And ye shall be as one which shall be counted -- and acceptable unto the School of Light -- "enlightenment." So shall ye be blest as none others.

* * * * *

The words which I use are for thine own sake. While I need no word to convey Mine meaning unto the ones which have given unto Me their heart, hand and head, they shall hear and understand Mine intent. They shall know as I know; we shall communicate mind to mind.

Let us speak again of the new heaven and the new moon. This is but the beginning of this revelation, for ye could not bear the fullness of it.

The moon shall remain within the place of its berth, while the "after-birth" shall fall back. This undeveloped object shall be brought to its maturity in due season and become a mystery unto thy earth science. They shall be mystified, for they have not known that which We know -- that which We are now revealing unto them. Them which shall believe and investigate shall be as ones the wiser, for We shall give unto them as they are prepared to receive. By the time the sleepers awaken, these things shall be known unto thine scientists.

For this do we labor, that none be caught off- guard. There are ones now within flesh which shall be as prepared to follow in the way I point. These shall be the new scientists which shall expose the foolishness of thine present ones. For they, these present scientists, have not seen from our point of view. They have not seen the whole -- they see in part only. They which are prepared to enter into the XTX shall see the whole -- not in part. Our equipment is so far advanced of thine that it is beyond man's (of Earth) imagination. For he is blinded by his own finding and opinions, even unto his exploration of space. He has not learned that which is hidden up from him. Therefore, there shall be many surprises for the next generation. These, the next generation, shall go out into the firmaments without great heavy, noisy, cumbersome gadgets which shall be outmoded for the coming generations.

I say this day: Oh ye fools -- ye unknowing ones -- art thou so foolish as to give of thine energy and effort to reach the ultimate? That ye be the foremost to accomplish what? What shall it profit thee? For ye shall not enter the "forbidden" places with thine intent -- for it is not pure! It is NOT pure. Therefore, ye shall not plunder the secrets of the Cosmos -- this is the law.

Heed ye well, oh man of Earth! For I have spoken the word, and it shall be heard, heeded, and obeyed. Thou shall not enter into the secret places of the Cosmos. The way of man is not Mine way. They are short-sighted -- blinded by their opinions -- preconceived ideas. They are an impatient specie; they are for the most part egotistical, foolhardy and rebellious. I ask of them naught which is not for their own welfare -- their freedom. While they labor and sweat -- give unto themself the "bitter cup", I stand ready to give Mine all -- Mine love -- Mine wisdom -- Mine energy -- that they be lifted up -- that they be delivered unto their rightful estate.

Wherein have they reserved for Me a seat in their chambers of justice -- yea, within their temples of worship? Whom do they worship? I ask, whom dost thou give credit for thine Being? Wherein hast thou been comforted in the time of stress? Wherefrom cometh thine fortune? Wherein shall ye find solace in the time of stress, thine time of weeping? For it shall come! It shall come! For I have said it, and it is so.

122

Let thine thoughts be turned to thine Source -- from which all thine blessings come. Be ye as one to remember that which I have said unto thee in these documents. Yet these words shall be followed by yet stronger and of more revealings. Be ye not hasty to lay aside these, Mine words, in denial. For the day of reckoning draweth nigh.

The time was when man of Earth was one with his Source -- knowing of his relationship -- of his heritage. Yet he went into darkness, forgetting the fullness of his own free will. He hast forgotten his place in which he had his beginning -- his rightful estate. Now We of the Lighted Ones come that ye, O man of Earth, be reminded again -- and prepared to claim thine inheritance, willed unto thee of the Father-Mother God -- thine Source of Being. Art thou willing to arise from thine bed, wherein ye have dreamed thine dreams of illusion -- and them which have followed thee, to torment thee? What hast thine fancies profited thee? Where hast thine illusions profited thee?

Now We, which are sent from out the Inner Temple of the Living God, hast come nigh unto thee that ye be quickened -- that ye awaken unto thine true estate. Art thou prepared to receive that which we bring forth, that ye be delivered up? Art thou willing to follow where I lead thee?

I ask of thee, can ye truly answer Me, "Yea, Lord"? Consider well before ye make answer, for it is serious business. When one gives his pledge and defaults -- betrays himself- I say he is the worst of traitor. So be it upon his shoulders. He alone is the loser -- the saddest of the lot.

Wherein is it written that the Earth shall be as one free from her suffering? is it not part of the renewing -- the cleansing -- the bringing

123

forth the new heaven -- the new earth? Is it not said: All things shall be made new? Why is it so strange that I say it at this time? I am alert to the timing of these events. Therefore, I see and know.

Now it behooves Me to make these things known unto thee. Such is Mine part at this time, for it is of the greatest concern unto us of the Council. While we are speaking in many ways -- in many tongues -- unto many earthlings of these things, it is our intent to arouse them and bring them in, wherein they may be prepared for their greater part. So let these portions, small as they be, be unto thee one, and a part of thine awakening, or preparation for greater revelation. It shall profit thee -- so let it be.

Be ye alert unto that which goes on about thee, for there are about the land these ones which would rob thee of thine inheritance, such as ye have no knowledge of. These are called the dark forces. "What are these?" I hear ye ask. These are the ones which have <u>not the mind which is in Me</u>. They know not that there is "Light". They are unaware of their eternal being -- they are of another realm. For the most part, they are humanoid and of darkness. They may not know what "evil" means. They are primarily without soul. These are not to be feared -- <u>just understood</u>.

Yet it is wise to be alert to their activities, for they come into thine midst and make confusion. Yet, is it not said and recorded, "Seek ye first the Light of God and nothing of darkness shall come nigh unto thee"? I have said it many times. Have ye taken note?

For there is much confusion brought about by these dark ones. Now let it be understood that there are ones of <u>thine own realm</u> which have misused the energy for their own satisfaction and mischief. Yea, even unto the <u>so-called</u> Christian, which comes under the domination of the Anti-Christ. Know him? Hast thou heard of him?

Now let this be made clear. <u>The Anti-Christ is the one which hast the will to set aside the plan which hast been designed to free thee of all bondage and suffering</u>. He hast sold his soul for to hold bondage the children of Earth. It is not of any value at this time to elaborate upon this subject. Yet, I say unto one and all, a word to the wise should suffice!

Let it be sufficient that which I have given unto thee within this little book, for yet another shall come forth of a different tenor which is designed for thine enlightenment. Be ye as ones prepared for to receive it. For this is it designed, that ye be ready.

Hast it not been given unto thee in thy books of yesteryear that I should return unto thee? Hast thou not heard that which hast been said many times, in many languages? He is Come, the "King of Kings", the "Lord of Lords"? For this ye shall be as ones to listen, for 'tis I, He which is come, as one of thee, as man.

I walk amongst thee as man. Yet be ye not deceived -- have no opinions about Me or Mine plans. For ye know Me not - neither that which I do. I am of the Light. I Am that I Am. I am not bound by flesh and bone. I am free -- unlimited am l. I go and come at will. I can, and do, take any form which suits Mine purpose, for I know no boundaries or limitations. Be ye as the one which can see and know that which I shall reveal unto thee. Be ye blest to know Me as I Am.

* * * * *

125

Sori Sori: Say unto them, as I would, that there shall be greater winds - greater fires -- greater floods -- greater droughts. These shall add great suffering unto the plagues -- plagues of every kind, too numerous to mention. The ones which survive it shall be as ones blest, for they shall be as ones which hast atoned for their misused energy.

It is truly seen that there shall be all kinds of beings which shall be brought forth from the lower regions, which shall be strange and unknown. These shall be fierce and untamed. Many shall be from the pits of darkness -- fearsome to the sight. They shall invade even the dwelling places in search of food. Some shall be as the beast of the field, Others shall be as part human, and these shall be the worst of the lot.

Be ye prepared for such as shall come upon the Earth. I say, ye shall be as ones prepared for to stand tall, firm and unshaken. For it is no time to lose thine composure or to fear for thine life. I say, prepare thine self, for surely it comes!

By Mine own hand shall ye be as one protected <u>when ye give unto Me thine all, whole heartedly</u>, and there shall be protection from harm. For ye shall be brought out. Now, be ye not misled, for I say: When ye are prepared to receive Me ye shall be brought out.

Is it not written, "Ye shall be brought out before the day of sorrow"? It is true. Yet ye shall be as one true unto thine own self. Fear not. Panic is an ugly thing where reason fails thee, and danger rides upon the wind. Blest art these which stand stalwart and fearless. These shall be the victors. So be it and Selah.

* * * * *

Sori Sori: These words have been chosen for a purpose: Of bringing unto the attention of ones in need of greater simplicity of communication -- and the true meaning of certain expressions, so often used by the thoughtless ones. Now I say unto one and all, there are things which shall be recalled unto the ones of a mind to learn of Me, the Lord God.

By Mine own hand shall I cause these things to be revealed unto the one which comes as a little child, pure of heart and clean hands -- with PURE intent. These words are of Mine own plan, designed for to hide from the bigot and hypocrite Mine jewels -- purposely hidden are they. I say to the pure of heart, seek and ye shall find. It is so written, and it is so. So be it and Selah.

* * * * *

Sori Sori: There are ones which have their hand in the till of the poor laborer which is bowed down with the responsibilities imposed upon him. These which sit in high places of government are the Anti-Christ. These are ones which hold to the precept, "every man is responsible for himself and his family." Do ye find them in the temples of worship? Whom do they follow? Art they the authors of freedom? I say not.

While I say unto one and all, THERE ARE TRIED AND TRUE MEN WHICH SIT IN THE SEAT OF JUSTICE FOR THE GOOD OF ALL -- these are to be commended. These shall find their reward. Yet they, too, come under the yoke. These shall stand before the bar of justice also. One shall receive the Crown of Victory. The other shall wear the cross of shame, that of the traitor.

While the traitor has his hand in the till, the laborer's children hunger. These I shall address: Mine children shall come unto Me, and they shall hunger no more, for they have learned their lessons of suffering and their compassion great. So be it they shall no more be born of woman. These have earned their freedom. While the "tyrant" is yet unaware of his part, he hears not Mine call, His part shall be hard indeed. For he hast not reckoned with the law of life, nor that of the man-made law. He hast not honored such as "Equality" or "Brotherhood".

Now it is the time of sifting and sorting -- each shall be weighed in the balance. He shall be dealt with as he hast portioned out unto himself. Wherein shall the tyrant find peace? Wherein hast he given comfort unto the hungered and sick? I ask him, hast thou prospered of thine own effort, that thine fellow man be comforted, fed and clothed? Hast thou given shelter to a homeless child? Hast thou dried the tears of the orphaned? Can ye, the tyrant, answer Me truly? Be ye as one to come forth, as one before the bar of justice, and answer Me. <u>Remember</u>, this is the day of accounting.

* * * * *

Sori Sori: I shall speak unto the generations unborn -- for these, Mine Words, shall not pass away. These are designed for all men, be he in the Earth this day or hundred years hence.

There shall come among thee this day, ones which sift and sort the traitors from the "tried and true". They which are the traitors, the "Anti-Christs", shall be put in their rightful place prepared for them. They shall be shorn of their positions -- yea, of their power to hold slaves -- the laborer which he hast given the "bitter cup". He, the traitor, shall learn well the lesson of compassion and love. He shall atone for all his misused energy - "tis the law of justice and mercy.

Now, I speak of the oppressed and downtrodden -- the <u>tried and true</u> which hast been as one which knows the law, and abides by it in faith and humility; the ones which have given unto Me credit for being that which I am. For they have kept the faith. They have given of themself when all others failed him. When he hast been naked and hungry, he hast remembered Me and Mine precepts. He hast walked in Mine footsteps -- for that he shall be remembered. Blest are they which remember Me and obey Mine precepts. For this shall I give unto him as he hast earned -- that which is his by divine right. So be it as the Father wills, and so shall it Be. And Selah.

There shall come one from out the place wherein I am which shall walk as man among men of Earth -- and he shall carry within his hand the sword of truth and justice. He shall sit in council with the heads of nations and direct them which hast the will to hear and co-operate. These shall be as the ones which shall be the trail-blazers for/ to the Golden Age -- the age when the tyrants shall no longer sit in the "scorner's seats and hold the people hostage.

Them which demand freedom for all -- these trail-blazers -- shall be as ones which come as ones sent. Yet, perhaps, ones may have been unaware of their beginning; yet they are true unto their calling. They fear naught. They are of one purpose/intent, come into the world of darkness that it be cleansed of the darkness, "evil" which hast held the unknowing child of Earth in bondage. These ones of ill intent shall be banished from the places of government, and there shall be justice for all. So be it and Selah.

Is it not written, and truly so, that there shall be heads of governments roll? Is it not so? So be it as it is written. Yet, it is also written that these which have betrayed themself shall find justice for each and every deed, every act of injustice, with his fellow man. There is no escape from the law which is just.

Then it is foreseen that they which have come with "holy intent" shall bring about the freedom which the Father hast willed unto his children. For this is the day of liberation. For this give unto Him, the Father, thanks for His grace and mercy.

* * * * *

Sori Sori: Let there be understanding of these, Mine Words. When I speak of Him, the Father-Mother God, it is not meant a gender such as man of Earth. It is a manner of speaking which shall not be equated unto, or with thine of this, thine realm. There is confusion in interpretations.

Therefore, I say unto each and every one, be not concerned with that which is beyond thine own understanding. I speak that ye might be enlightened of the things which ye can comprehend. Some may have their memory restored. Some may hear that which they are prepared for to hear. Others might see, while others hear. Some might feel to know. Therein are different ways of knowing. Yet I say even these are but parts -- each know but parts of the whole.

I have said that there is a School wherein ye/they shall learn that which shall bring thee into the fullness of thine memory, or thine Godhood -- thine Sonship -- thine inheritance. Hast thou remembered that which I have said? Let it be so, for that ye shall receive in greater measure.

* * * * *

Sori Sori: Since we began these communications, many new experiences have come unto our attention. For example, the one which hast been unsavory, to say the least - - hast it not? Yet it is just the beginning. Watch, listen, and give unto "them" nothing they can use against thee. For they, the press, are merciless. Yet the nation shall be better for its presence.

While there are ones which think to hide their nefarious schemes, I say there shall be no place to hide, for there is no hiding place. They shall be exposed -- So be it. For they have, and are, weaving their own web. Foolish tho they be, they are not exempt from the law -- be they void of "good judgment" or evil intent. When they are found out -- exposed -- they cry and try to cover their "bad judgment". So it is!! So it is. And so it shall be, again and again. While "We" see them weaving the web, we endeavor to warn them. "They" are so intent upon their schemes, they hear us not. Therefore, each man or woman shall drink his own cup of "bitter tea". So be it, they shall savor to the last bitter drop.

* * * * *

Sori Sori: "Freedom." Freedom is that which is earned by laying down that which becomes guilt -- thy burden of past guilt -- that which one considers a wrong action -- which hast not been atoned for or corrected -- possibly buried within the closet -- yet not forgotten, truly. This "burden" can be heavy -- haunting -- until discovered and corrected.

131

Be ye as one to remember, for it is that which shall free thee from the past which is buried. This is called Karma, is it not? Watch thy haunting dreams -- analyze them. Ask for Light, that they be made clear. 'Tis the better way to clear the past. Forgive thine unknowing while ye are searching the record. A word to the wise should be sufficient.

Let us proceed with the governments of the world. Yea, it is as an open book unto "Us" which sit in Council for the "good of all men". For thy good is our good, is it not?

This is the time of sifting, sorting the tares from the wheat. We are at the crossroads. We see both ways -- what hast been and that which is to come. While man hast free will, he hast set in motion that which shall run its course. We see the fruits of his sowing, and for this can we see the fruits of his reaping.

Be ye as one which knows that the law knows no favorites. No man is so wise that he can hide his intentions from Us, thine Guardians and Benefactors.

We say unto the ones which hold such responsible positions, be it State or Church: Be ye as one honorable in all thine dealings, for ye shall be held accountable for all thine actions. Every word that proceeds from thine mouth and its intent is recorded.

This is our part -- to make known unto the candidate these precepts as they give their oath. For they are responsible unto Us even as they pledge their honor to uphold their constitution. For that was our part which we had in bringing forth thy Constitution, that it be upheld and honored by the patrons of "freedom and justice for all." O foolish man,

132

how blind and stupid to betray thine self for a poor counterfeit penny. I shall not belabor this subject herein this little space, longer. Yet the subject shall not be overlooked, or forgotten.

Now let us speak of the way of man and woman. Hast they given themself the "bitter cup"? I see it so! They have each had a part in the reaping of their sowing. Their harvest shall be one of great sorrow, for there hast not been the honor due each for the other. Man hast held woman in bondage -- yea, long -- too long. While woman hast now in this day fought for her freedom, she hast, for the most part, forfeited her divine right -- that of femininity -- her heritage -- mothering, nurturing the offspring -- the home.

Wherein hast she won? Wherein hast she fulfilled her part willed unto her? For it is said, "Ye shall go forth and bring forth thine children in <u>love</u> and <u>honor</u> -- honor thine husband." Hast thou, woman, honored thine gift of the Father -- yea, thine husband? Hast this union been one "made in heaven" -- or hell? This shall suffice as a quick reminder herein. While it is not forgotten, all things are recorded as they happen -- I might say, for example, on "etheric tape." Know Mine meaning?

Now let me refresh the reader's memory. Hast thou remembered the time ye cried out for Mine assistance? What happened? I ask of thee, what happened? Hast thou forgotten so soon? Did ye believe that ye were the deliverer of thine own? Did ye say one word of thanks? And to whom? To what did ye give credit? Do ye remember?

Did ye take the gift so freely given and go thine way? Accounting it unto thine friends? What think ye this reprieve? What say ye stayed the hand of the grim reaper? Be ye as one to recount these experiences. It shall be of great benefit, should ye be one which hast been neglectful.

133

I say, none so thoughtless as the one which forgets his Benefactors which give assistance where needed. Remember their assistance is given for a purpose – not without a divine purpose. Shall I say more herein?

Just a reminder to these which overlooked their blessings upon their journey through the Valley of Earth.

* * * * *

For this moment let us give our attention to the ones which suffer -- the ones which have not known their "higher self," of which they speak so fluently. These have gone their own way, in their own will. They, for the most part, thought themself wise -- sufficient -- and very much their "own man", so to speak -- fearing naught -- caring not for their kin or kith.

I say that it is for this that they be brought up short -- that they which suffer shall languish in pain. They shall account for their deeds -- the suffering they have caused others -- until it is atoned for, unto the last jot and tittle. Hear that which I say! For this does concern each and every one as a reminder.

Be ye as one which hast a mind to comprehend Mine reminders herein. I have spoken in cryptic terms, yet no mystery do I create for thee. Blest are they which give attention unto Mine reminders. For they shall take note of them and profit thereby. So be it and Selah.

* * * * *

Sori Sori: This shall be Mine word unto each and every one which finds this little book. It is for a purpose that I have chosen this one, which is

134

"Mine hand made manifest," and each word is carefully given that it finds its mark. Therein is profound wisdom in Mine method, for each word is weighed with thee in mind. I have seen that which shall be the fruit of Mine effort. I see some reach -- yea, reach for Mine meaning, and that is well. For unto them it shall be given when it is a sincere seeker for truth.

Unto the one which is filled with self-righteousness and criticism, these words shall be sealed up. They shall be filled with scorn and denial -- so be it. Let it not be of any concern unto thee, Mine own. For ye shall know on what ye stand (the Rock) which I Am.

Be ye no part of them which are the Anti-Christ. For I have called thee out from them, and ye hast heard Me. So be ye as one which can endure their foolishness with patience and silence -- non-resistance! Let them have their say. I need no defense. For I am Mine own author and I know well Mine subject. I need no critic; I ask no favors. am sufficient unto Mine needs.

Mine needs are for Mine people which are Mine "men in the field of action" wherein they need the materials which shall be used to place these, Mine words, within thine hand -- yea, and to feed the hungry. Think ye that ye are ones alone? I see the need for such as Mine little ones need. I am mindful of them, yet they, too, come under the LAW. I cannot be their burden bearer -- when they have chosen to create them.

Such is Mine part, to know the law and reveal it, or recall it to their memory. Then assist the ones tried and true to do that which they have chosen before they entered into this present plane of existence, I know where to place them for to do their work; I know their needs -- be it material substance or spiritual. I can and do sift and sort -- gather together, then sort out -- then scatter for a purpose -- even though they know not Mine Plan. Be ye not deceived; I have a Plan. When one walks in his own will, he stumbles and falls. Then he may blame Me - - or take upon himself the blame, and pick himself up and proceed with his lesson which he hast learned. Then I shall remember him, and hear his plea for help.

* * * * *

Sori Sori: Where shall I find thee when I call? Where hast thou been when I hear the babies cry? Hast thou heard them? Hast thou given thot of these little ones which have been deprived that which ye enjoy?

The life which so many waste in useless pursuit of pleasure. Hast thou been within these places wherein these little ones are destroyed by the ones which deliberately tear them from the mother's womb? Know these ones? Hast thou heard the cry of the unborn? Wherein have ye turned thine head that ye see not the horror of it? Art thou one to sanction this bloody carnage of the innocent?

Wherein hast thou given thought of the cause of their suffering? Think ye they do not suffer? O, ye sleepers! Or do ye know that which is done in the time of thine unknowing?

I say unto one and all, "thine 'sins' shall find thee out" is not a platitude - 'tis the law -- what ye sow ye shall reap. Hast thou learned the meaning of this expression?

When a soul hast been brought forth, then deprived of its material sheath, it is the responsibility of each one which hast part -- Willing or unwilling in such as is portioned out unto the unborn. Think ye there is no pain involved in this, the worst of all crime? I say, there is a law:

136

"Ye shall not kill". Hast thou heard this, or have ye considered it thine privilege to take that which ye cannot give?

O, ye unenlightened ones! I ask of thee, list unto Me, for it is of great concern unto us of the realms of Light. There are ones which have come unto us scarred from that unholy deed thou hast committed against these little ones. Know the responsibility, in this thine time, shall come -- thine time of reckoning shall come. For none escape the law.

I say unto thee, be ye alert and see that which ye do. Know that which is involved within this "evil", for think ye not that there is no evil involved! For it is the work -- the prompting of the dark force which prompts such action and gives unto thee to say it is the right of any one which-soever enters into such activity!

Could ye but see the cloud of blackness which hangs about these traps of death, ye should be as ones bowed down with remorse and fear. Fear -- yea, great fear shall follow thee, and ye shall cry out for mercy.

I have spoken that which ye shall come to hear, listen to, and heed. For the time of accounting is at hand. So be it, it behooves thee to hear that which I am saying. I need not say more in this, Mine little book. For there are many places, many voices raised against thee and these evil practices which ye try to justify. There is no justification!!

* * * * *

Sori Sori: There be ones which hast the will to come unto Me -- yet there are the ones which would bar their way. For this I speak unto thee of the "dark forces", for they are about in full armor. Be ye as one appraised of their ways. Put not thine foot in their trap, for it is cunningly set and well baited. It is seen that which they do to entice thee into their traps.

They first flatter then -- entice thee with that ye desire -- promise thee great finery -- comfort, pleasure -- whatever ego craves. Then they leave thee when ye cry for relief from all that ye have brought about by thine foolishness and "gullibility". Thine burden becomes heavy, and painful the responsibility -- more than ye had calculated. Now ye are left hanging. "Where turn now?" Hast this been thy lot? Ye shall find it very sad, should ye not understand the way of the dark ones.

Be ye aware. For this am I speaking thusly. Keep thine own counsel. Ask no man for his advice -- how to reach the School of which I speak, for he, too, is without the knowledge. Be as one prepared to give unto Me thine whole heart, head and hand, and I shall lead thee safely. So be it and Selah.

Question not of another that which I will do. For no man knoweth Mine Plan. So be it I shall reveal, bit by bit, as ye are prepared to receive. So be it and Selah.

* * * * *

Sori Sori: Now it is come when we shall speak of the time when blood is running in the street. Hast it not been foretold? And I say unto thee, it is but the beginning. This shall be a reminder of Mine word unto them which yet sleep. The time swiftly comes when every nation shall come unto its knees. Then shall come one which shall sweep clean that which hast been polluted. This shall be the "end time" so long spoken of. There shall be the war of Light and darkness which no man can image.

There shall be ones which come from afar -- which bring with them such power that no man hast known, which shall sweep clean that which hast been polluted. For this shall this great and powerful army of Light be sent of the Father. This shall be recorded within the annals of time, the greatest of all events of the Earth's history. So be it and Selah.

Let this be Mine testimony unto all which have the mind to comprehend these sayings of Mine, for unto them am I speaking. Yet there are sleepers which shall sleep on. While they shall awaken in the place prepared for them, they shall have their memory blanked from them. They shall have nothing. By their bare hands shall they scratch the soil for their substance. They shall have no memory of their previous existence -- as tho they had none. These shall be the ones which have scoffed and put aside the many warnings sent forth from the Realms of Light. These are the "traitors".

Be ye as one which hast the will to comprehend that which is coming forth, that ye be prepared for these times of sorrow.

Awaken! Awaken! all ye sleepers -- for this am I crying from the mountain top! Hear ye Me, for it is for Mine love and compassion that I am come to alert thee unto thine own responsibility. Then when ye have alerted thine self, I shall do Mine part for thee that ye perish not.

* * * * *

Sori Sori: Wherein is it written that the time is at hand "when every knee shall bow and every tongue shall confess Mine power; Mine truth"? So shall it be. For I have come that the Earth shall be as one free from man's pollution, and hast it not been polluted unto saturation?

139

So be it the time is at hand when great armies shall clash -- and the streets shall be filled with blood. Yet it is but the beginning. For we of the heavenly Host shall be as the power which shall bring order out of chaos. Be ye as one which shall come through the flame of purification unscathed, unharmed. So be it as the Father wills.

* * * * *

Sori Sori: While there are ones which have their hands in the till, I say there are ones responsible for the part assigned unto them. These are "tried and true". These ones shall be commended for their work. Their effort shall be unto them great gifts. Their reward shall be great, for they are the ones which shall be the seed for the new root race.

These shall bring forth the greatest generation yet born upon the Earth, for they shall be the pure of heart and filled with Light. So be it that there shall be a New Earth and a New Heaven, which shall be their abiding place. There shall be no darkness therein. These ones which are the seed for the New Earth shall be as the Sons of God. For they have been reborn -- born of the Light of the Father-Mother God.

Now I say unto one and all, form ye no opinions of that which I say, for ye could not image that which this event entails. For ye know not that which ye do here and now: How could ye possibly understand such a great cosmic event? It is not even expected of thee. Yet it is well that these, Mine words, be brought forth at this time, that they be engraven upon the mind of the ones prepared for that which they shall be given to do. For their memory shall be returned, and they shall remember their covenant with Me, the Lord God. So be it a great day of Revelation. For this I am bringing forth that which is wise and prudent, that each one might be prepared for that which shall come about.

Thine mind cannot conceive of the things which shall be done in the name of "religion". These I choose not to enumerate herein. Yet I say that I am prepared to prove Mineself. For I shall bring forth a mighty force to meet the <u>foe</u> on his own ground.

This shall be Mine battle cry: Awaken! Awaken! Awaken! all which sleepeth. Dost thou hear that call -- that DEMAND? Yea, demand it is. For the sleepers shall be removed into yet another place prepared for them. And their sleep shall be long and restless. Be ye as one to stir thine self and get thine self up and about the business of the "Time" which is now. The business is thine awakening.

Let Me give ye another parable. While ye are drinking -- dancing -- giving forth thine energy unto the forces of destruction, art thou aware that the day of accounting is upon thee? What think ye of tomorrow? Hast thou heard that which I have said in this little book of reminders?

Unto them which have denied Me and Mine word (the traitors) shall be as ones caught up short of their course. They shall come to know they have been misled by the false one. He hast led them to the brink of destruction and forsaken them.

Now, I hear them cry as ones trapt. What say ye, the captive? What would ye have Me do? Would ye have me deliver thee out? What say ye? Give unto Mine question some serious thought. For it is a grave situation that ye face. Be ye aware of the time. It is come when ye shall make clear thine decision. 'Tis no time for frivolity or indecision, for it is said, "Time waits for no man".

Think ye I am playing games -- or making of Mineself a fool? What think ye of Me? Know ye that which I am? Hast thou given thought of

Mine words -- the work I have done on thine behalf? Or, hast thou given unto these things thought? <u>Serious</u> thought? Should ye be one to scoff and mimic, I would give unto thee this word: There are many now crying in darkness - languishing -- remorseful that they did not listen. Pity are they. Their waiting shall be long and hard.

For this day let it be said that there are ones which come unto Me scarred and fearful, yet I know them -- that which they are. They have forgotten their Source, yet they are prepared to go all the way with Me. They are weary of their illusions and forgetfulness. These I shall raise up, and give unto them as they are prepared to receive. These shall have their memory restored. Then they shall rejoice: "IT IS COME! IT IS COME! FREEDOM AT LAST -- O, SWEET FREEDOM!"

Mine hand I extend unto all. Yet not all choose Mine way. I have said, I bring none against their will. While I see them crying out for help, they know not from whence it comes. They have forgotten Me -- even tho' they have walked with Me in the Eleusian fields.

* * * * *

Sori Sori: While this little book is but a reminder of things yet to come and that which hast come, I say it is sufficient to provoke thought. So be it; it is given with the greatest of love and compassion for all humanity, both the ones which are awake and giving their all that the sleepers awaken. The sleepers, too, are held within Our radiance, for they are but the unknowing ones. For this are We showing our hand in fellowship.

Now it is come when We of the Mighty Council shall show our self in great strength. Be ye alert unto that which goes on about thee, for that ye shall become awake. 'Tis the beginning of thine awakening. So let it be for this do We make known our self. In unison do We come -- with love to all.

I am one of the many which stand by for the good of all. Let it be as the Father wills. SO SHALL IT BE.

* * * * *

By mine own hand hast this little book been penned. It is mine testimony unto one and all, that I have heard that which hast been said -- that which hast been done.

For that have I taken note of the ones which are prepared to follow where I lead them. For that, shall these which hear me and follow me, be brought into the School of higher learning. These shall be truly blest. So be it and Selah.

'To All which follow the Light'

-- Finished --

June 12, 1989

Sori Sori: "This, it is finished. Now we shall do a new thing. A new project shall be given unto us which shall be as new. This, too, shall be separate from any other that I have given unto thee. Now for this ye shall need a plan which shall take thee unto a place ye have not been, and there shall be one which shall accompany thee -- which knows his way around. This shall be for the good of all. Now when these books -- these which are yet within thine hands -- are printed and back within thy hand, ye shall go into the place I shall send thee as Mine hand and foot made manifest -- and give unto thineself credit for being that (Mine hand and foot). For are we not One -- of one mind -- one purpose? The purpose is to awaken the sleepers -- so let us work in unison and it shall be well.

* * * * *

Sori Sori: This shall be our next project. When these books are finished, ye shall go forth unto the place where I shall indicate. This place shall be new unto thee, yet ye shall not be a stranger unto them there. Ye shall be as one prepared, for as soon as the books are finished a Plan shall be brought forth for to give direction.

When the books are finished, ye shall go into this place which shall be strange and new unto thee. Yet the ones therein shall know thee and be prepared to receive thee. There shall be no need for any luggage, for every need shall be supplied. Fret not thine self about that which ye shall do or say, for I say ye shall know that which ye shall do or say.

* * * * *

Sori Sori: While it is of little consequence that they have the books in the day ahead, or in the next month, it is expedient that it is finished by the end of thy summer.

Each book is designed for to serve Mine Plan. Therefore, no changes of any sort shall be made. This is for to serve a purpose that I have not as yet revealed. I have said it shall find its mark -- so it shall.

For now, this day ye shall be as one which has the time for thine own self, thine personal affairs. On the morrow we shall give energy unto some new things. Be ye as one with Me and thoughtful of our communication, for it is now come when there shall be great action. So be it and Selah.

Recorded by Sister Thedra

www.ingramcontent.com/pod-product-compliance
Lightning Source LLC
Chambersburg PA
CBHW071500070426
42452CB00041B/1946